GIFT PLANTS

Houseplant Beauty All Year Long

GIFT PLANTS

HOUSEPLANT BEAUTY
ALL YEAR LONG

JACK KRAMER

Drawings by Michael Valdez

G.P. PUTNAM'S SONS   NEW YORK

Contents

Introduction: Keep Them Growing

Today, plants are expensive, and gift or florist plants, those that you receive or perhaps buy for yourself at the peak of perfection, are especially dear. These beautiful plants generally last only a few weeks or a month before they wilt or die, but they can decorate your home or apartment for years if you know what to do with them when you first receive them and how to care for them in the future so they remain handsome plants.

There is no reason why an azalea or poinsettia given at Christmas should not grace your house or apartment for the next year with colorful bloom. The Easter cactus and geraniums you get at Easter can also become permanent residents, as can the lovely gardenia, and the popular gloxinia, that is usually in florist shops in fall, is a splendid all-year addition in the home. None of these plants (and many other fine florist plants) are difficult to carry over or grow-on if you know how to do it, and that's what this book is all about.

Other florist gifts such as dish gardens and terrariums, are also discussed with full details on how to care for these arrangements and what to do to make them last for many years indoors. And of course from original mature gift plants, we also tell you how to get free plants from cuttings, division, or by rooting offshoots.

Gift plants are really a gift from the giver and from nature, and with this book in hand you can realize this harvest—a bounty of enjoyment for you and your home not only for a few weeks but all year long.

JACK KRAMER

GIFT PLANTS

Houseplant Beauty All Year Long

to Vickie,

It's very nice to have you for a friend. And don't eat to much while you're staying at home. (IHE..IHE.IHE.). Hope you're likes this book and good luck.

A friend,

Jacqueline

3/2 81

1

Gift Plants

The gift plants most likely to give us pleasure at home are the flowering ones that provide so much color. But in the last few years, handsome foliage plants have also become ideal seasonal plants. The term "seasonal" suggests that a plant will last only a month or perhaps a season—say three months—but most gift plants can survive for many years if you know how to take care of them. If you know how they were grown in commercial greenhouses for seasonal sale, you will know what conditions these gift plants require. And what you do with a plant as soon as you receive it is another consideration. A plant's first few days with you can be the difference between its surviving a long time or lasting only a short while. Finally, *where you place the plant* indoors the first few weeks will help to determine whether it grows and flourishes or just exists.

How Gift Plants Are Grown

The flowering and foliage gift plants that have been grown to peak form by florists and nurserymen are the finest examples of the horticultural craft. These greenhouse-grown plants, which are necessary to the economy of the florist

13

Chrysanthemums are favorite gift plants and provide beautiful indoor accents almost anywhere. The decorative container adds to their beauty. *(Photo by Matthew Barr)*

trade, are given optimum growing conditions to get the plant to you in top shape. Plants have had excellent humidity, plenty of water and forced feeding, and good ventilation—all the advantages of a greenhouse. And although the plants have been grown in warmth by day, at night they have been subjected to cool temperatures of about 60F; oddly enough, plants need this change in temperature to prosper.

African violets are favorites with gardeners and make charming table accents. Here clay pots of violets have been set into a brass planter out of direct light but close enough to a window to furnish some bright light. Once accustomed to indoor light, plants can be moved to more intense light. *(Photo by Joyce R. Wilson)*

14

The forced-feeding program enables buds to open and bloom fully, thus making the gift plant really a gift, a gift from nature, encouraged by man to the peak of its form. All this beauty is lovely, but forced feeding also means that after a plant blooms, a rest period of some kind, a few weeks or a few months, is necessary so the plant can regain its vigor for another season of beauty. Here lies the fallacy of the gift plant: Overfeeding can occur because when you get the plant home you want to prolong its perfection, and so you feed, water, and pamper it just when it really wants to be alone. How you handle the plant on arrival and what you do to it and for it are vital to its well-being.

On Arrival

Remember that most gift plants are grown in somewhat cool conditions without excessive warmth or direct sun, which burns most plants. Do not immediately plunge the plant into a hot, sunny place; such plants as poinsettias, cyclamens, chrysanthemums, and azaleas will die overnight if you do.

Well-grown geraniums are a pleasing sight. The ivy varieties can be grown outdoors or indoors for spot decoration. Keep them out of intense light. *(Photo by author)*

Plants that have been in the home for a few weeks can be placed at a window to provide a handsome accent such as the gloxinias and calceolarias shown here.
(Photo by Max Eckert)

The best procedure is to put the plant in a somewhat cool (60F) shady place near a window receiving west or north light. Or put the plant on a living-room table; just be sure that for the time being no direct sun hits the plant.

Most people want their gift plant on display, which usually means the living room. Rather than risking the window position, where sun can affect the plant adversely, put the plant in a spot with some artificial light. An ordinary incandescent lamp (a reading light) is fine, but be sure it is far enough away so the heat from the lamp does not harm the plant. Make sure the plant is in an area with good air circulation because few plants will grow in a stagnant atmosphere.

Step-One Basics for Good Plant Health

Generally, care for the plant—watering, humidity, temperature, and feeding—should be minimal for the first few weeks the plant is at home. All that is needed is routine watering; just keep soil evenly moist. (Later you can start a routine care program; this will be discussed in Chapter 3.) Most likely your plant will be in full flower or in bud. The plant in full flower will last longest if you keep it as cool as possible (heat quickly desiccates blooms). The plants in bud need a different treatment to get buds to open. Mist the general area of the plant so a fine mist of water reaches the bud. This softens the outer casing, enabling the bud to open. Often, in low humidities

Lining an areaway, an excellent place for new arrivals, are pots of chrysan-themums. The light is bright, but not intense and the plants add much beauty to the scene. *(Photo by Max Eckert)*

A fine begonia makes a handsome gift for anyone and is equally at home on table or desk. This plant is beautifully grown, symmetrical and in bloom. *(Photo by Matthew Barr)*

plants will drop flower buds or simply not open, mainly because of dry air. Once the plant is in full flower, start reducing moisture; get it ready for its rest period.

Foliage plants are easier to handle indoors than flowering kinds. Keep soil just evenly moist, and occasionally spray leaves with water to keep them looking good. Most foliage plants will want to rest after their forced-feeding program at the wholesale growers' greenhouses.

The poinsettia is perhaps the most popular gift plant. Recent hybrids have excellent keeping quality and stay in color for weeks. *(Photo by Roche)*

18

2
Containers

Gift plants are pretty pictures and so should be suitably framed; this means a handsome container. There are dozens of pots and tubs, and some knowledge of them will make it easier for you to have your gift plants looking good all the time. Certainly, a well-scrubbed clay pot is acceptable, but the decorative cachepot, jardiniere, or wicker basket puts the plant on display. The container is just as important as the plant and should be given consideration because it is the total unity that makes the handsome scene.

In addition to the containers just mentioned, there is a choice of acrylic or plastic pots, bonsai pots and dishes as well as one-of-a-kind pottery. If you want unique decoration from your gift plants, you will suit them with appropriate housings that complement both the plant and your apartment or home.

The plant you get from the florist generally will be in a terra-cotta pot and wrapped with aluminum foil in a seasonal color. Terra-cotta pots harmonize with most room colors, but ornamental pots may look better in your room's decor or more dramatically display your plant.

Years ago there was little choice in containers, but today

The standard clay pot has been a favorite for years. It comes in many different sizes and is well suited to all plants. *(Photo by Matthew Barr)*

there is a container to fit practically any room interior. Just what kind of container you select depends upon the room itself, where the plant is, and the kind of plant.

No matter what kind of container you choose, try to use one with drainage holes; this allows excess water from soil to escape rather than becoming stagnant in the soil, which can harm plants. Containers without drainage holes require very careful watering and even then, no matter how careful you are, after a period of time, water is apt to accumulate at the bottom of the soil.

Terra-Cotta

As mentioned, gift plants usually come in a standard terra-cotta pot. There are dozens of other handsome designs, however, in this material. The following are examples.

Italian: The standard border is modified to a tight-lipped detail.

Venetian: Barrel-shaped, with concentric rings pressed into its side.

Spanish: Outward sloping sides; flared lip.

Three-legged pots: Bowl-shaped.

Cylindrical: Cylindrically shaped sides.

Bulb pans (azalea pots): Deep and squat.

Simple white glazed containers are elegant and appropriate for these trained ivies. Note that all the pots are the same shape and color, which creates a uniform pleasing effect. *(Photo by Max Eckert)*

This handsome tapered pot has a simple design and makes a fine container for plants. Always be sure that pots have drainage holes. *(Photo by Matthew Barr)*

Each type of terra-cotta pot has a definite character; select the one that best suits the room interior, and make your selection with the plant in mind. A branching plant looks best in a bowl-shaped pot, but a vertical plant is more appropriate in a cylindrically shaped container. Rosette plants are handsome in Spanish pots; Italian pottery seems to suit most plants.

Ornate pots and urns for plants are available today in many shapes and sizes. These shown are particularly appropriate for plants. *(Photo by Matthew Barr)*

Cachepots and Other Ornamental Pots

Cachepots were originally designed as coverups for terra-cotta pots. The porcelain cachepots, generally splashed with fruit and flower designs, are especially pleasing, and the ones with a footed base have a note of elegance. Others are delicately etched with a Greek border design.

Urns and jardinieres are other fine containers for plants and come in many different sizes and designs. Almost any plant looks good in a handsome jardiniere. Glazed Japanese urns are stunning in that special place which needs color. Blue glazed tubs are attractive with branching plants.

Chinese ceramic pots, generally glazed in blue or green hues, are handsome and ideal for foliage plants. Some are extremely ornate; others are simple. Brass and gold-leaf tubs also make any gift plant a special plant.

Square and tapered boxes of stone make dramatic containers for plants. They brighten any indoor area. *(Photo by Matthew Barr)*

Plastic

Since there is some confusion about plastic pots, clarification is necessary. A plastic pot may be of flexible polyethylene. Growers use these especially for hanging plants, (These are the thin brown or green containers used for hanging plants sold at supermarkets, drugstores, and discount houses.) These inexpensive pots also come in other colors; the colors have improved recently, but basically the flexible plastic pots are not aesthetically pleasing to the eye. The pots are suitable for kitchen plants, but to my way of thinking they are not decorative enough for other areas of the house. Also note that a heavy plant invariably topples over in a lightweight plastic pot. Rigid plastic, a better quality of plastic, has more substance and durability and looks somewhat better than the flexible plastic pots. Rigid plastic pots come with matching saucers and can be used if necessary, but they are still not an ultimate choice of container for a plant.

In a separate category, but also called plastic, is rigid, clear acrylic. Recently introduced, acrylic pots have great elegance, look good in the home in almost any area, and most plants look quite handsome in them. They come with matching acrylic saucers and impart a clean simple character to a plant. These pots are slightly more costly than the flexible plastic ones, but they are worth the extra money.

Remember that plastic pots retain water longer in the soil because plastic is a nonporous material. This can be good or bad: If you are neglectful about watering, it is an advantage, but if you water frequently, soil can become soggy, which is harmful to plants.

Cover-ups

If you have an unsightly or unattractive pot, perk it up by using decorative cover-ups. (You should never plant directly in cover-ups; insert the potted plant into the cover-ups.) Cover-ups include rattan, wicker, and wood containers. The most popular container at the moment is the handsome wicker bas-

A simple brass planter is used for African violets. Most brass planters do not have drainage holes, so the pots are merely set inside the planter.
(Photo by Joyce R. Wilson)

ket for hanging plants. The wicker baskets come in several sizes, and some have an ingenious metal insert that supports the plant and a drip saucer. Other wicker or simulated rattan containers are also available, but they do not have the wire insert. When you put a potted plant in them, invariably they drip water, and in time the wicker rots from excess moisture. Seek the wicker baskets with metal inserts for best results. Some cedar and redwood baskets also have metal inserts to hold the plant, but others have solid wooden boards that act as a watertight enclosure, Flexible bamboo or wicker cover-ups simply wrap around the pot, adding some decorative flair. Some are real wicker, but most are made of simulated plastics, so shop carefully before making a final decision.

Glazed Pots

These very decorative containers come in lovely bright colors and have a fired-on shiny or mat-finish glaze. Some manufacturers do not put drainage holes in these pots , others do, so select carefully. The only drawback of glazed pots is that the fired-on glaze prohibits gradual evaporation of moisture from the soil; waterlogged soil results. Keep this in mind when watering your plants.

Another type of glazed pot, and one I like very much, is the

25

painted terra-cotta container. A painted shiny finish is applied to the standard pot. The porosity of the pot is somewhat reduced, resulting in slower evaporation of moisture than from an unglazed terra-cotta pot.

Pottery and Glass

Pottery includes one-of-a-kind or mass-produced ceramic pots in a dazzling array of shapes and sizes in lovely finishes. These unique containers have great appeal. Colors vary from brown to black to combinations of blue and blue-green, and because the shapes are so unusual, these pots are fine choices for a special plant.

Pottery containers are sold at plant boutiques or local craft shows and generally have drainage holes. Some are glazed, but others are not—the choice is really a matter of personal taste and what blends well with your home.

Glass containers in the shape of a cylinder have nice appeal. They do not have drainage holes, however, so watering can be a problem for the home gardener. I once used these containers. The plants did look elegant but did not do well, probably because I have so many plants that I did not have time to really observe and tend the plants in glass as I should have. So if you have only a few plants and patience and time use glass containers; your plants will undoubtedly thrive.

Saucers

You definitely will need something under your potted plant to catch excess water and to avoid staining tables and floor surfaces. The conventional drip-tray is a saucer that comes in various depths and diameters. The most popular saucer is the terra-cotta one, but because terra-cotta is porous, eventually water and moisture will seep through and stain wood. Some of these saucers are now being made with cork insert mats; they work far better than the conventional terra-cotta ones. The glazed or painted saucer is also satisfactory for use under a pot.

26

3

Caring for Gift Plants

Chapter 1 outlined some step-one basics for keeping plants in good health after you first get them. Now for step two: what to do once plants have adjusted to your home conditions and how to keep them growing. There is a vast difference between these two programs, one that I hope to clarify here. Following is information on soils, feeding, and repotting and how to care for your plants. Soil is the vital ingredient for all plants confined to pots, although feeding and repotting are equally important. None of these steps is difficult; they just take some basic considerations and, most of all, some good common sense.

Soils

Now that the plant has become accustomed to your indoor conditions, it is time to think about soil. When you get your gift plant, you do not know what kind of soil the grower used. Many times gift plants are grown in soilless mixes that have very little or no nutrients but are lightweight, which is why they are used. You can tell whether the plant is in ordinary soil or in a soilless medium: Lift the pot; if it is lightweight, a soilless medium was used. If it is a soilless mix, in a few

Soils for plants come in many kinds and under many trade names. Don't buy just anything; be sure you get the best soil possible for your plants. *(Photo by Matthew Barr)*

weeks repot the plant in fresh soil. Soiless mediums must be fed regularly, which is a chore.

If the plant is in soil, there is really no way of telling whether all the nutrients in that soil have been depleted by the plant. If they have been, the plant needs feeding; if the soil still has nutrients, it does not need feeding. Added food will only harm your plant. So again, in a week or so repot the plant.

It may seem bothersome to repot the plant in fresh soil, but it is worth the brief time it takes because often the container the plant comes in does not complement interiors or does not suit your personal tastes.

There are so many packaged plant soils available that the average person has a hard time determining just what to use. There are soils especially for African violet, others for citrus, still others for azalea, and so on. The best thing is to buy a package marked houseplant soil. But because the package is closed, there is little way of knowing what is inside. To further complicate matters, packages generally are not transparent, so you cannot see the soil's color: A good soil is rich black-brown. Finally, the nose test—good soil smells like (of) humus—is also impossible to do because of the package. What to do? Squeeze the package as you would a loaf of bread; if it is pliable and spongy, assume that the soil inside is good. This is the best you can do to test packaged soil.

28

Packaged soil is not cheap; a hobby sack can cost as much as two dollars and may contain only enough soil to pot one plant, although the outside of the package may state *for four or five plants.* What is not stated is that this refers to plants in small six-inch pots—your gift plant may be in a twelve-inch pot. Generally figure one package per plant. Packaged soil also comes in fifty-pound sacks, which is more economical but hardly feasible for the apartment dweller. Lugging soil is difficult in a large city.

If you can, buy bulk soil; this is the soil the nursery uses because it has all ingredients in it. Bulk soil should be porous and feel crumbly. Remember that bulk soil is very difficult to transport. When I was younger I bought bulk soil in shopping bags and carried them, bag by bag, up two flights of apartment stairs. It was worth the effort because I knew it was the finest soil I could get.

Repotting

As mentioned, wait a few weeks until you repot your new plant. Then select a suitable container, one neither too large nor too small for the plant. The container should never be out of proportion to the plant.

Repotting a plant has to be done only once a year, so take the time to do it right. Repotting should entail as little shock to the plant as possible. First tap the sides of the old pot against a wooden table or cutting board to loosen the root ball. Now lay the plant on its side on newspapers on a table, and try to slide the plant from the pot. Grasp the crown of the plant with one hand, hold the pot with the other hand, and gently tease the plant from the pot. Jiggle the plant until it becomes loose. Do not pull the plant out or the roots may rip. When you have the plant out of the pot, crumble away some but not all the old soil. Try and keep the root ball intact to some degree.

Now cover the drainage hole of the new container with a shard (a piece of clay pot), and fill the pot with about one inch of gravel. If the pot does not have drainage holes, have holes drilled in it at a glass store. Growing plants in containers with-

This lovely garden room relies on gift plants such as cinerarias for color. Note that the plants are in distinctive containers and have been recently repotted to assure good growth. *(Photo by Max Eckert)*

out drainage holes is tricky because a soggy soil can damage plant roots. Scatter a few charcoal chips into the pot. Now insert a mound of fresh soil and center the plant. If it is too low, add some soil; if it is too high, take out some soil. Once the plant is in position, fill in and around it with soil to one inch of the pot rim. Push the soil down around the collar of the plant with your thumbs or a blunt wooden stick. Tap the bottom of the pot to settle the soil, and then firm soil again with your thumbs to eliminate all air pockets. Water the soil thoroughly; in a few hours water it again.

If the plant will not come out of its existing pot, break the pot with a hammer rather than pull out the plant and ruin it. (The pot pieces can always be used as drainage material in new pots.)

Watering

The most frequent questions asked me at lectures deal with watering plants. It is not so much *when* you water plants or *how* you water them, but *how much* water to give them. While I give watering hints for plants in future chapters, here are some general suggestions to help you help your plants:

When you water plants, really water them; be sure excess water drains from the pot. Sparse watering results in dry pockets of soil and roots must reach for water; some will never get it.

Generally, water plants in five-, six-, or seven-inch pots three times a week in spring and summer, twice a week in fall and once or twice a week in winter, depending upon how much artificial heat you have in the area. The more heat, the more water. For plants in larger pots (which retain moisture longer than small ones), water plants twice a week all year except in winter when once a week is satisfactory.

Plants in very small pots (two-, three-, or four-inch pots) will have to be watered every other day, probably all year.

Usually, most plants should have an evenly moist soil all year except in winter when they can be barely moist.

Some plants (and there are few of these) need a thorough

This is an exceptionally well-grown Jerusalum cherry; it is symmetrical, well pruned and trained. *(Photo by Roche)*

soaking and then should be allowed to dry out before being watered again. This fact is noted in future plant descriptions, when this is the case.

It is a good idea to use tepid water for watering rather than icy-cold water which can shock plants.

While some experts say to water plants only in the early morning, I find that there is little difference in plant growth whether I water the soil in the morning, afternoon, or in the evening.

Don't worry about the quality of the water; if you can drink it, so can the plant.

If anything, under water rather than over water. More plants are killed by over watering than by any other single cause.

Feeding

Gift plants have been heavily fed before you get them to encourage flowers or lush growth. After its initial adjustment to

32

your home conditions and eventual repotting in fresh soil, the plant will need no feeding for several months. Fresh soil has adequate nutrients to last a plant many months, and additional feeding might harm it.

When nutrients in the soil are used up, however, it is time for a feeding program. But feeding should be done intelligently, never haphazardly. More is not better; less is often the wisest course. A plant can absorb food only when it is in the growing state, which is generally in spring or summer (most plants rest in fall and winter). During the growing period, plants should be fed every other watering with a weak solution of plant food.

Most plant foods are composed of nitrogen, for good general growth; phosphorus, for stem growth; and potassium, to keep plants disease-resistant. These elements are listed on the package in percentages, for example, 10-10-5 or 20-10-5. A 10-10-5 is a good general fertilizer for all gift plants.

Plant foods come in granular or soluble forms or are made for foliar feeding. Granular foods are sprinkled on the soil, and then the plant is watered. Soluble foods are mixed with water and applied to soil. Foliar foods are mixed with water and sprayed on plants. The granular foods are the most convenient because no mixing or spray equipment is needed.

Too much food will result in an accumulation of toxic salts that can kill plants, so use plant foods moderately. And always follow these five feeding rules:

1. Never feed ailing plants; they are in no condition to accept additional food.
2. Never feed dry plants; soil should be moist.
3. Do not feed plants in winter to try and force growth; it will kill them.
4. Do not use plant foods on plants such as ferns and orchids; they react adversely to additional feeding.
5. Do not use plant foods on newly potted plants; they have not adjusted to the transplanting shock, and food can harm them.

Another example of a well-grown plant is this compact azalea, handsome from all angles. *(Photo by Matthew Barr)*

Once or twice a year use a fish emulsion food. This contains many necessary ingredients and can do wonders for tired plants. It is available at suppliers.

A note here about specific plant foods which seem to be appearing in numbers. Quite frankly, standard plant foods already mentioned are very satisfactory, and there is little sense in paying extra money for special food for African violets, or cacti or philodendrons.

Grooming

Many people complain that their plants do not look good. This is a needless excuse. If you groom your plants occasionally—cut away dead leaves and errant stems—and provide minimum culture, your plants will look good at all times, not just for a few months. Grooming also helps prevent insects and disease. Dead or decaying leaves contribute to fungus diseases starting in plants and to an accumulation of insects.

Washing the leaves every month or so with a damp cloth helps to eliminate any insect eggs that foliage may harbor, and a good shower in the tub or at the sink always refreshes a plant.

Do not be afraid to cut away dead leaves or, for that matter, live ones if they are getting leggy. Cutting will not harm the plants and can help to stimulate new growth. I always cut back my hibiscus after the blooming period to keep it healthy; it comes back with a flush of new growth a few months later. Citrus and most shrublike plants also appreciate this grooming.

Keep the soil of the plant free of debris and decayed leaves. The soil should be clean at all times and not full of litter. This simple procedure takes but a few minutes. Pots and containers also should be kept sparkling clean. It is important to remember that gift plants are on display and thus should always be in peak form.

Ailing Plants

Because of incorrect culture, some plants may suffer, exhibiting symptoms of wilted leaves, limp stems, and a general look of illness. This may be due to over watering or not enough water, or perhaps the plant is in a draft. For sick plants it is wise to have some out-of-the-way areas where they can recuperate and regain strength. I find that an unheated but not freezing area is ideal, such as a pantry or a basement or even a garage that does not get too cold. When a plant is recovering, trim it somewhat, keep soil barely moist, and make sure there is ample circulation of air (but no drafts) and some light but not intense sun. Keep temperatures about 55F. Plants should stay in the "recovery room" for about a month or until they start showing signs of better growth; then they can be returned to their permanent place in the home.

Never throw away plants that look dead, such as orchids. Some species of orchids simply shrivel up for a season and then suddenly flourish. This is natural because many plants need a resting period, that is, less water and cooler temperatures.

4

Preventing Trouble

Keeping a plant in peak health is the best way to prevent problems because insects and disease rarely attack healthy, well-established specimens. But insects sometimes do infest a plant, or disease strikes. However, you can get rid of insects and diseases, usually without using poisons. Simple observations and hand picking of insects can prevent infestations, and grooming, which means clipping off dead stems and leaves, will prevent diseases.

Recognizing Symptoms

If your plant becomes ill, ask yourself the following five questions:
1. Is the plant getting too much or not enough water?
2. Is the plant getting too much heat?
3. Is the plant in a draft?
4. Is the plant getting too much feeding?
5. Is the plant getting too little or too much light?

If you answer "no" to all these questions, start watching the plant. Look for such culture or disease symptoms as yellow or streaked leaves, soft and brown stems, or foliage that

37

just falls off. If the plant exhibits none of these poor culture or disease symptoms and yet still does poorly, it may be infested with insects. To help prevent insects, spray and mist leaves with tepid water to remove insect eggs and spider mites before they hatch.

Leaves

A clean and healthy plant has lively, fresh, green, good-looking foliage, never discolored and streaked. If your plant's leaves do not look "right," check the following list of symptoms and culture, disease, or insect causes:

Leaf Symptoms	Possible Causes
Brown or yellow areas	Incorrect feeding; sun scorch
Yellow or white spots	Leaf-spot disease
Leaf drop	Thrips (insects); over watering
Brown edges	Anthracnose (fungi) disease; over watering; salt damage
Curled	Salt damage; thrips
Dried and brown	Under-watering; not enough nutrients in soil
Smaller leaves than mature ones	Lack of nutrients
Sticky substance	Usually aphids or mealybugs

Black sooty coating	Mildew
Silver streaks	Thrips
Eaten at edges	Slugs, snails
Coated white	Mildew and molds
Gray or yellow	Under fertilizing; mold
Deformed	Salt damage; mites
Transparent areas	Thrips

Stems and Crowns

Many fungus diseases (see next section) start at the crown of a plant. If caught quickly, they can be remedied, but fungus can kill a plant if it is not treated. Also, many insects start their colonies in stems and leaf axils, so inspect these areas carefully. Stems should be healthy and firm, with good color; plant crowns should be solid, never turgid or soft.

STEMS AND CROWN SYMPTOMS	POSSIBLE CAUSES
White or powdery stems	Mildew; molds
Limp stems	Over watering; poor drainage
Stems covered with clear, sticky substance	Ants or gathering colonies of aphids
Stems do not develop	Underfeeding; lack of water

39

Soft stem growth	Crown and stem rot disease; over watering
Soft crowns	Crown and stem rot disease; over watering
Brown or gray crowns	Rot; fungus

Plant Diseases

If plants are well cared for, they will rarely be bothered by diseases. But if diseases do strike your plants, you should know what to do; you do not want your expensive plants ruined by fungus or mildew, especially when a little knowledge can help you save them.

Ailments that strike plants are manifested in such visible symptoms as spots, rots, and mildew. Many plant diseases exhibit the same external symptoms, so you must be able to identify the specific disease to ensure positive remedies.

Too little or too much humidity or too much feeding can contribute to disease, but diseases are caused mainly by bacteria and fungi. Bacteria enter through a plant's natural minute wounds and small openings. Once inside a plant, bacteria multiply and start to break down plant tissue. Soft rots, leaf rots, and stem wilts are diseases caused by bacteria. Animals, soil, insects, water, and dust carry bacteria that can attack plants. If you touch a diseased plant and then a healthy one, you may infect the healthy plant, so be extra careful if you are sure a plant is diseased.

Fungi, like bacteria, enter a plant through a wound or a natural opening, or by forcing their entrance directly through plant stems or leaves. Spores are carried by wind, water, insects, people, and equipment. Fungi multiply rapidly in shady and damp conditions rather than in hot and dry situations; moisture is essential in their reproduction. Fungi cause rusts, mildew, leaf spot, and blights.

Mealybug is in evidence at lower left on this pepe-romia; the white cottony insects can be seen in leaf axils. *(Photo by Matthew Barr)*

Chemical Disease Preventatives

Fungicides, chemicals that kill or inhibit the growth of bac-teria and fungi, come in dust, ready-to-use, or wettable pow-der forms, as well as water-soluble forms that have to be sprayed on a plant. If necessary, try some of the following fungicides, but use them carefully:

1. Captan is generally safe and effective for the control of many diseases.
2. Ferbam is very effective against rusts.
3. Karanthane is highly effective for many types of pow-dery mildew.
4. Sulfur, a cheap standby, controls many diseases.
5. Zineb and Benomyl are good for many bacterial and fun-gus diseases.

41

Insects

A plant lightly infested with insects can be saved by chemicals or old-fashioned remedies like a laundry soap and water spraying. But you *must* know what insect is attacking your plant. Most common houseplant insects can generally be seen: aphids, red spider mites, mealybugs, scale, snails, slugs, and so on. If you cannot identify the insect, pick it off, kill it, and mail it to your county agricultural agency; they may be able to identify it.

Aphids

Aphids (plant lice) are carriers (vectors) of mosaic and other virus diseases, so you *must* eliminate them. If you cannot see these insects, observe the plant: *It loses vigor, may become stunted, and leaves may curl or pucker as juices are drained out by the bugs.*

Aphids generally hatch live young (nymphs) in the spring or autumn. Typical aphids are black, red, green, pink, yellow, lavender, or gray; the young aphids may differ in color from the adult. These insects are pear-shaped, small and soft-bodied, with a beak that has four needlelike stylets. These daggers pierce plant tissue and suck out plant sap. Aphids also excrete honeydew or sugar; this excretion is a great breeding ground for the growth of a black fungus known as sooty mold.

Scale

Scale are appropriately named: Their tiny and oval-shaped bodies are covered with an armored shell. The wingless females insert their mouth parts through a leaf and start taking in sap. They will stay in the same spot on a plant their entire lifetime, molting twice and laying eggs or often bearing live offspring. Male scale have elongated bodies and eventually develop wings; they look like gnats when mature. They prefer to attack stems, although they also go after leaves. Thus, *plants infested with scale will show leaf as well as stem damage.*

A close-up of aphids; these insects attack all kinds of plants. However, well-grown plants are rarely bothered by pests. *(Photo USDA)*

Scale are the easiest insects to fight because they are easy to see and identify. Plants will generally be bothered by the hard-scale types, but some soft-scale types also attack plants. Scale come in many different colors and prefer new rather than mature growth.

Mealybugs

Mealybugs are related to scale. These bugs, which have soft, segmented bodies dressed in cotton wax, leave cottony accumulations in the leaf axils or on leaf veins. Young mealybugs are smooth-bodied, crawling, oval-shaped, light yellow, six-legged insects. They insert their beaks into plant parts to get sap; *as the sap leaves your plant, your plant wilts.* The youngsters develop the cottony waxy covering once they start feeding, moving slower day by day. But although you may think mealybugs are not moving, they are. Like aphids, mealybugs produce a honeydew that is a breeding ground for sooty mold fungi and attracts ants.

Male mealybugs, unlike the females, develop flylike wings. Soon after they mate with the female they die. Some mealybugs can become as large as one-eighth inch in diameter.

A close-up of mealybug on a cactus. Early detection can save plants from such infestations.
(Photo by author)

An Azalea tip that has been destroyed by either red spider mites or fungi. Watch plants closely and remove any dead or infested leaves immediately. *(Photo by Matthew Barr)*

Red Spider Mites

Red spider mites are yellow, green, red, or brown tiny, oval-shaped bugs. They have long legs and are almost impossible to see on a plant. The webs these bugs spin is a clue to their presence on a plant.

The two-spotted mite is the worst plant offender. Spider mites injure plants by piercing the leaves and sucking out cell liquid. *Foliage turns pale and may become stippled around the injured parts. If the infestation is not checked, the leaves turn rust-red and die.* Plants may become covered with silken webs that the mites make as they move from area to area.

Because of their tiny size, spider mites are difficult to see and thus eliminate. Also, their rapid reproduction rate (100 to 200 eggs per female per month) and habit of using lower-leaf surfaces (where you are not apt to look) as their breeding places makes them particularly hard to see.

Thrips

These chewing, tiny, slender insects have two pairs of long and narrow wings. Their mouths have "tools" that pierce or rasp leaves. Adult thrips are generally dark-colored and most active in the spring or summer. Female thrips lay eggs on stems or within plants' tissues. The transparent larvae hatch within two to thirty days, depending upon the species, and

45

start sucking plant sap. So you must be alert and get them early. After a few days the larvae change their skins and become tougher. Some thrips are active flyers, others just jump around, and still others hardly move at all. *A silver sheen among the leaves is a sure indication of thrips.*

Chemical Insect Preventatives

There are so many insecticides and so many trade names that you must know something about them. Chemical insect preventatives are sold in granule, water-soluble, and powder or dust forms. The granular type (systemics) is the easiest to use; it is sprinkled on the soil and water is applied. The water-soluble types have to be sprayed on plants with special sprayers. I do not think powders or dusts are necessary for home use. Besides being convenient, systemics protect plants from most sucking and chewing pests for eight weeks, which means you have to apply them only three or four times a year. The principle behind systemics is simple. They first dissolve in the roots, and then they are drawn into the sap stream as a toxic liquid. Thus, when sucking and chewing insects start eating the plant, they are poisoned.

How to Use Chemical Insect Preventatives

Follow directions on the package to the letter each time (more than one dose is necessary to eliminate insects completely). Keep poisons out of reach of children and pets; use a high shelf or locked cabinet and do *not* leave the key where a child can reach it! Malathion is a good all-purpose chemical that does not have an accumulative effect. Always follow these other six rules:
1. Use chemicals in well-ventilated areas; outdoors is best.
2. Use sprays at proper distance marked on package.
3. Do not use chemicals on ferns.
4. Never use a chemical on a bone-dry plant.
5. Never spray plants in direct sun.
6. Try to douse insects if they are in sight.

46

TRADE OR BRAND NAME	INSECTS	REMARKS
Malathion	Aphids, mites, scale	Broad spectrum insecticide fairly nontoxic to human beings and animals
Diazinon, Spectracide	Aphids, mites, scale	Good, but more toxic than Malathion
Sevin	All types	Available in powder or dust forms
Isotox	Effective on most but not all insects	Systemic; toxic but effective
Meta-Systox	Effective on most but not all insects	Systemic; toxic but effective
Black Leaf 40	Aphids and sucking insects	A tobacco extract; relatively toxic but safe for plants
Pyrethrum	Aphids, flies, household pests	Botanical insecticide; generally safe
Rotenone	Aphids, flies, household pests	Often used in combination with Pyrethrum

Aerosol bombs: Generally sold under different trade names. Can harm leaves if sprayed too close; also can irritate your lungs. Do not use any outdoor spray for indoor plants.

Old-Fashioned Insect Remedies

Old-fashioned insect remedies are perhaps not as thorough as chemicals, but they are safer, and with them there are no noxious odors in the house. Try these six effective standbys:

1. Handpicking. Use a toothpick.
2. Soap and water. A solution of one-half pound of laundry soap (not detergent) and water works well on insects such as aphids and mealybugs. Spray or douse mixture on bugs; repeat applications every three to six days for three weeks.
3. Alcohol. Alcohol on cotton swabs applied directly to the insects will effectively remove mealybugs and aphids.
4. Tobacco. Good against scale. Steep old cigarette tobacco in water for several days. Repeat applications several times.
5. Water spray. Wash away insects frequently with strong force.
6. Wipe leaves frequently with damp cloth to eliminate eggs before they hatch.

5

Displaying Gift Plants

Plants serve many purposes in the home, but their main advantages are that they decorate and complement surroundings and provide cheer. There are innumerable ways to use gift plants indoors to enhance room interiors. It is just a matter of getting suitable containers for them and using color effectively in the rooms. Just where you place plants does make a difference; decide upon a specific area for your gift plant, that is, where it will be the most handsome. Logically you will want plants on windowsills, desks, or tables for accent, or, if they are large (floor plants), for guiding traffic or acting as natural dividers. Large plants can be also used like furniture, occupying a bare corner or adding loveliness to an empty window wall.

Windowsills

People make the mistake of putting any plant on a windowsill, but sometimes this can cause the death of the plant. Many plants react adversely to strong sunlight and fluctuating temperatures, which are most apt to be near windows. Some plants, like begonias, can take it and be placed anywhere, but plants like gardenias will not tolerate such conditions. The

Hydrangeas at a window. Use many plants rather than a single one for a real display.
(Photo by Max Eckert)

size of the plant will also dictate its placement: Large plants obviously will not fit on windowsills, so medium- or smaller-sized gift plants like African violets, gloxinias, and cyclamen are the best for north or west windowsills.

In natural light windowsill plants will need more water than plants away from good light, so provide sufficient moisture. And because these plants are apt to be in hot conditions during the summer, mist the foliage frequently to keep plants cool (more plants are killed from excessive heat than from cold).

Turn plants on windowsills so they will grow symmetrically rather than lopsidedly—a quarter turn once a week works fine for most houseplants.

A window-box full of colorful geraniums decorates this breakfast area. Note the hanging basket of campanulas.
(Photo by Max Eckert, Christiansen, Designer)

50

On a table, a bromeliad holds cut flowers to create a special effect. *(Photo by Max Eckert)*

Tables and Desks

Use plants on tables and desks as you would a vase or a dish: as an accent. Because your table or desk will most likely be away from light, plants *must* be those that can tolerate a shady place: kalanchoes, philodendrons, and begonias. Do not stretch your luck by trying chrysanthemums or hibiscus, because these plants do need some sun to prosper.

Use decorative ornamental containers like cachepots or distinctive pottery. Terra-cotta pots, fine for most other places, do not work well on a table or desk; the earthy color is handsome, but the style and color of a porcelain cachepot or pewter container is much more in keeping with contemporary or traditional furniture (see Chapter 2).

Containers like cachepots often come with attached saucers, so water stain is no problem, but for other receptacles use handsome saucers under the pot to protect furniture. Small embossed mats under the saucers will further ensure that water does not stain tables or desks.

It is fine to use one unique plant like *Neoreglia carolinae* as a table or desk accent, but you might also want smaller plants

51

like cyclamens or gloxinias. If you do, use two or three pots as a grouping to create a lovely scene. Do not keep plants away from light too long; put them back in natural light every few days to make sure they continue to grow and remain pretty.

Floors

Plants on the floor are apt to be gift plants like hibiscus, poinsettias, and gardenias (to three feet). Floor plants are handsome, but they look even better on small platforms or wooden pedestals. Most of the larger plants will provide a vertical accent to a room, thus adding dimension. Never put the plants too close to a chair, table, or window because foliage tips might be bruised; always allow some space between the leaves and the object they are near.

One large plant in a room is fine, but often another plant somewhere in the area acts as a fine counterbalance and creates a more pleasing arrangement. For example, a tall plant can be used in one area, with a somewhat bushy branching plant like citrus in another area nearby. This will provide both vertical and horizontal thrust in the room.

As with the table and desk plants, use a saucer and mat under the pot so there will not be any water stain on floors (this is not necessary if you use plant pedestals with saucers). Standard clay pots are attractive at floor level, but for something quite dramatic, insert plants into a Chinese jardiniere or a gold-leaf tub. Remember not to pot directly in the ornamental container; just set the potted plant inside, and use sphagnum moss to dress the top and hide the rim of the pot.

In Rooms

There are numerous ways to use gift plants indoors as special accents, but some tricks about grouping, arranging, and which plants look best where must be considered. For example, in the living and dining rooms you need plants that really put on a show, so that is where you should use flowering

This fireplace is highlighted by a group of phalaenopsis orchids; other plants complement the room. *(Photo by Max Eckert)*

plants with lots of color. Azaleas, gloxinias, and cyclamens are stellar decorations and should be used in groups rather than a single plant which, in a large room, creates a spotty effect.

Grouping plants is not difficult; simply use three to five pots of the same plant in a row in the same kind of container. This creates a flow of color that carries the eye across a room. If the idea of the single-pot effect bothers you, you can use a handsome brass planter, about thirty-six inches long, and set pots in this on a bed of gravel. This floral-pot arrangement works well and looks handsome in a living or dining room and adds that note of living color to an area. If there is a long window expanse, such a row arrangement can provide a pleasing horizontal dimension. If you would rather not place plants at floor level, consider small pedestals. Try a box arrangement of pedestals of different heights to carry the eye up and down and thus create interest.

A single specimen of a large plant such as a hibiscus or a bromeliad can also offer fine decoration in a living room. In this case the solitary plant is used to furnish accent and provide beauty. Such plants should be in ornamental containers on pedestals or on floor platforms, which you can make yourself. Gardenias, with their lush foliage and white flowers, can also be used and make a fine statement in a room. In fact, any large branching, full plant can create the desired effect. A plant in a corner is fine, but why not use it as a substitute for a piece of furniture? Try a single large plant behind a sofa, on a table, or even in the center of the room, with smaller plants placed around it (to guide traffic).

In the kitchen, stay with smaller plants like lovely African violets or distinctive begonias. A row of pot plants at a window or under a counter shelf equipped with artificial light can do a great deal to brighten the kitchen. Near windows and above the sink are other fine areas for the smaller plants to put on their show. By the way, in the kitchen, plants have an advantage: There is always high humidity due to the steam from cooking or washing dishes.

Bathrooms, too, deserve some plants. A few fine gift plants

like cyclamens or cinerarias can enhance the looks of this room immeasurably. The bathroom, generally a sterile area, needs living plants to somewhat soften severe lines. Generally, light from bathroom windows (obscure glass windows) is excellent for all plants because it is filtered, not too bright and not too shady, which is most beneficial for plants. Showers create additional humidity, so plants thrive, and although you may forget to water plants in other rooms, water is always at hand in the bathroom. (Keep a small watering can in the bathroom as a reminder.)

Here gloxinias are used as a centerpiece on a coffee table to bring color into the room. Plants can live several weeks in such a situation but should eventually be returned to better growing conditions. *(Photo by Max Eckert, Hudson Designer)*

All plants have uses in the home, but some are better than others for various purposes. The following list cites the more dependable and stalwart gift plants that can be counted on always to perform admirably:

Aechmea chantini. A large plant, to sixty inches; spreading rosette with dark green leaves banded with white, and tall erect flower stalk of red and yellow vivid bracts. A superb decorative plant.

A. fasciata (Grecian urn plant). An excellent carefree plant that makes a fine show. Grows to thirty-six inches; green leaves banded silver, and tufted flower crown of blue and pink blooms.

Azalea. Small-leaved, with cheerful flowers; makes a nice bushy effect when used in groups of three pots. The accent here is on color, if that is what is needed in an area.

Cattleya. Fine orchids, to thirty-six inches; some of the hybrids bloom twice a year, with large six- or seven-inch dramatic flowers. When out of bloom, return plants to windows.

Citrus. A wonderful assortment of fine branching trees that can be used as pleasant accompaniments in any room where a sculptural effect is needed. Most citrus are fairly undemanding and offer a great deal of color.

Columnea. A rather large hanging plant, with oval bright-green leaves and magnificent orange flowers once or twice a year. One of the best flowering plants for a garden in the air and always beautiful even without bloom.

Dipladenia amoena. The fine Mexican love vine cascades from twenty-four to thirty inches. A leafy plant, with grand shell-pink flowers; is at its peak in the summer months for almost any area.

Euphorbia splendens (crown-of-thorns). Definitely a table plant; grows to about forty inches. Branching, with tiny leaves and elegant red bracts. Looks good all year, even in a shady area.

Geraniums. Better than most people think for indoor beauty if you can keep them cool (55F). Grow several pots to an area for a mass of color. Plants rarely exceed thirty inches; if space is a problem, use miniature varieties.

Hibiscus. Easy to grow if you remember to clip it back once or twice a year after it blooms. Grows to about sixty inches and makes a fine treelike plant indoors. Many new varieties. Takes time to adjust, so do not get discouraged if it loses a few leaves at the start.

Trichocereus spachianus. A fine but large cactus (to six feet) with a candelabra shape. Almost impossible to kill, and lives a long time even in untoward conditions.

Zygocactus. Many varieties. Most are elegant, with pendant, succulent, scalloped leaves and bright red or pink flowers at tips. Does quite well in warmth or coolness but does need good light. Nice for hanging baskets or shelves. (See Chapter 7 for complete plant list.)

Bookshelves and Room Dividers

These areas are excellent places for smaller pot plants, especially trailing ones like the lipstick vine and dipladenia. Placed at corners, the trailing foliage covers the mechanism of the bookshelf or étagerè and makes a fine focal point in a room. Never put plants in the rear of the shelf; place them toward the front so they can be an extension of the vertical accent of the divider or bookcase. If possible, use one plant to a shelf at the same placement so you create a vertical column of green that suggests an outdoor scene indoors. (Merely placing plants at random on shelves will not create the beauty of the vertical arrangement.) However, a row of three or four plants on one shelf will also create a maximum decorative effect.

Ferns, which have become popular gift plants, are ideal for shelves and dividers because the pendant fronds cascade over the furniture, creating a softening effect. Avoid very large ferns and varieties such as Fluffy Ruffles or Rooseveltii; use the simple Boston fern. This plant and its varieties have fronds that are spaced apart, giving a lacy look, which is to be desired, rather than a mass of green.

A unique and highly effective way of decorating a stairway. Eight pots of chrysanthemums make the picture here. *(Photo by Max Eckert)*

Lighting Your Plants

Do not be afraid to use some small spotlights to accent your plants. Do not confuse accent lighting of plants with growing plants under artificial light, which is an entirely different thing. When placed strategically, lighting can act as a beautiful accompaniment to plants by silhouetting the leaves and casting lovely shadows on walls and ceilings. Spotlights on floors, aimed at an angle at the ceiling, concentrate light on the plant itself. This theatrical type of lighting does have a place in the home. However, do not go overboard with garishly colored lights or too many lights; be discreet and use a single lamp in good taste. A wide assortment of fixtures and lamps are sold at electrical supply shops. Always place the lamp at least thirty-six inches from the plant to eliminate any possibility of heat from the lamp burning the foliage.

6

From Indoors to Outdoors

Many of the gift plants—gardenias, hibiscus, citrus—definitely can be used outdoors in summer. In fact, most plants will benefit greatly from being outside because they absorb rain water and fresh air, thus getting completely revitalized for the indoor winter season. (Some plants are best left indoors; ferns and palms are prime examples because they can become very beaten by winds and severe rains.) But the real advantage of putting your gift plants outdoors is that they will serve as beautiful decoration for your garden, patio, terrace, balcony, or porch. You will need more than one plant, but if you have been frugal and cared for plants, you may have several in a few years. Or you can grow some of your own plants from those gift plants you have received, as explained in Chapter 10.

Putting Plants Outdoors

Select an outdoor spot that has some sun or bright light but which is also protected from strong wind and rain. And do *not* put potted plants on a balcony ledge or a similar place. Severe summer winds can blow plants over, and the heavy pots might fall on someone below.

This outdoor atrium, off a bedroom, is filled with
gift plants and makes a beautiful retreat. The light
is bright but not intense and plants grow lushly.
(Photo by Hedrich Blessing)

Generally, plants can be moved outdoors in May and
brought in after Labor Day. Plants like azaleas and poinsettias
demand outdoor culture to keep them going all year. If you
put plants in the garden, do not plant directly into soil. It is
better to just dig holes and sink the pots into them; there is no
sense in uprooting a plant for a three month period. However,
in areas of year-round temperate temperatures, direct planting is fine. Here in California I do plant gift poinsettias outdoors, but when I lived in a Chicago apartment, I placed my
gift plants on my porch for the summer.

Decorating the Outdoors

Gift plants can be used around pools, on decks, for walkways, porches and entranceways. There are innumerable places where they can add beauty to the scene in the warm months and then be returned indoors for the rest of the year.

But do not put plants just any place outdoors. Whether plants are on a patio or terrace, porch, or balcony, use a little thought in arranging your gift plants. Put them in groups where they will do the most for an area, generally in corners or near posts. Try to give plants some dimension when placing them so they will look better. Use inverted pots to raise a plant, and group three at different levels in a given area to create a very handsome scene.

Camellias in tubs spend the summer outdoors and winter indoors. Outdoor conditions suit most plants and refresh them. *(Photo by Matthew Barr)*

Primroses in simple white pots decorate a corner of a terrace and at the same time enjoy a delightful holiday in warm weather. *(Photo by Max Eckert)*

Around swimming pools, medium and small plants in terra-cotta pots provide color and also act as a barrier. Use leafy plants like gardenias or geraniums. At poolside, avoid cacti or some of the bromeliads that have spiny leaves. The best arrangement is perhaps a group of pots at a corner or in a straight row along one side of the pool. This adds dimension and color to otherwise barren swimming pool areas.

For deck greenery, almost any kind of gift plant in a suitable pot can be used. Again, groups of plants look better than a single specimen. Bromeliads provide leafy color; pots of chrysanthemums, lilies, or begonias are also stellar decoration. These can be randomly placed on the deck or patio or in specific areas to guide traffic.

Porches and entryways need not be barren either; even a few pot plants will dress them up immeasurably, so do consider strategic placement of plants in these places. However, do not impede traffic. For best results use plants as borders and edgeways, never in the center of a porch or entranceway. Plants at different levels offer a great spot of decoration, and small wooden pedestals or platforms will lend a unique look to a porch or entryway garden.

If there is wall space (my Chicago apartment had a brick wall as part of the porch), use the convenient wall brackets and clip-on pot hangers. Barren walls will suddenly become green ones, an especially handsome sight in the city. Indeed, with clever arrangements you can create a wall garden that you can enjoy in all seasons.

Because plants outdoors are in natural conditions, you will have to feed them copiously. Rains will naturally leach out any accumulated toxic salts, so there is little danger from overfeeding. Do trim and prune plants when they go outdoors to encourage fresh new growth.

Returning Plants to the Home

I do not normally recommend poisons for plants, but when you take your indoor plants into your apartment or house, it is a good idea to use an insecticide spray. Plants outdoors are

An array of colorful gift plants make this patio a handsome sight; cinerarias, azaleas—all kinds of festive plants are grown here. The pots are attached to the fence with clip-on hangers available at suppliers. *(Photo by Max Eckert)*

exposed to good climatic conditions, but they also face insects, so spray with Malathion before you return plants indoors. At this time it is also a good idea to wash pots and generally clean up the plant with a good grooming to get it ready for its indoor season.

Once indoors, your plants are liable to react as they did when you first received them—lose a few leaves, appear wan—because they are adjusting again. Do not panic. Just put plants in the coolest, brightest place you can; in a few weeks they will recover and grow better than ever. They have had a tremendous boost from their outdoor vacation, so even if you mistakenly mistreat and forget to water them now, most can pull through the darkest days of winter in fine fettle.

This small outdoor area is enlivened by the addition of pot plants; in winter plants can be moved indoors.
(Photo by Roger Scharmer)

7
Gift Plants From A to Z

This chapter is a list of the many gift plants available. I have tried to include as many as I know of, but no doubt I missed some that you may know. This is because of space, not choice. Specific growing instructions are given for all plants and I have also indicated whether plants are difficult or amenable. (A chart of these plants, with their basic requirements, appears at the end of this chapter, and in Chapter 8 you will find a list of bulbous plants.)

Aechmea fasciata (Grecian urn plant, bromeliad)

Known as carefree plants, bromeliads are members of the pineapple family. This species in particular has become the leader of the group as the plant most likely to be given as a gift (or found at florists). This very handsome vase-shaped plant has broad leaves banded in frosty white and pale green. The flower spikes appear in the center of the plant and grow to about twenty inches, crowned with tiny pink flowers. (The overall height of this bromeliad can reach three feet.) The lasting quality of the blooms—for two months—makes it a desirable houseplant.

This bromeliad needs little care. It will grow in any light

AECHMEA

condition, although a place with some sun is best. Pot plants in an equal mix of fir bark and soil or in soil alone. Keep the potting medium evenly moist all year, and the saucer under the plant must *always* have a supply of water. In other words, be sure to fill the saucer even if you forget to water the soil.

The plant appreciates repotting every year but will, if necessary, grow in the same pot for many years without undue harm except that growth will be slow. Once the plant blooms, it steadily declines no matter how you treat it. As it dies it puts out small offshoots at the base to perpetuate itself. These offsets, when they are three or four inches tall, can be cut from the mother plant and potted separately as new plants (see Chapter 10). Thus your gift bromeliad is really many plants in one: one plant can give you enough stock for many years.

If you have the choice of one gift plant, this should be it because it truly needs little care (even the worst gardener would have difficulty harming it) and is quite handsome.

A. chantini, large, and dramatic is also becoming popular as an indoor plant. It resembles *A. fasciata* but has bolder colors.

Aeschynanthus speciosa (lipstick vine)

This member of the gesneriad family has become a popular gift plant, probably because of its catchy common name of lipstick vine. When in flower it does resemble a vine of red lipstick tubes. Dark green leaves closely set on stems can cause trouble: Excessive moisture and shade invite mealybugs. I thin the leaf stems (a very unorthodox procedure) so I will not have to cope later with mealybugs.

With only minimal care these plants can really be gifts because they will stay with you for years. Every year repot plants so they will have fresh soil. Trim and prune them to keep them within bounds or they will get quite straggly. Plants do best in hanging containers in a place with good air circulation and bright light. Keep the plants well watered, and feed them at least once a month in spring or summer. Several new

ANTHURIUM

varieties have been introduced, some with brown flowers. But what you want is *Aeschynanthus speciosa.* Ask for it by botanical name.

Anthurium (flamingo flower)

This handsome tropical beauty has become increasingly popular as a gift plant because the flowering red spathe lasts for several months. However, beautiful as it may be, the flamingo plant is simply not that easy to rear indoors. It requires, unlike many other plants mentioned in this book, a very humid situation (at least sixty percent) and warmth. Never allow the temperature to go below 65F. Soil must be kept evenly moist, almost saturated at all times, and a good circulation of air is necessary.

The anthurium is a small plant, growing barely more than twenty-four inches. Those of you who want a challenge will find it in this tropical exotic. And although anthurium does need pampering, it is well worth the extra time because a healthy plant is a handsome spectacle. Give it that little extra care and it will be with you for years.

Azalea

These vibrantly colored flowering gems always make stunning gift plants. The variety Gumpo, which is a smaller type of azalea, is generally avialable at florists in January. Flowers may be red or white. The plants have a nice branching habit, neither too small nor too large, and look handsome in ornamental pottery in almost any place in the house.

When you receive an azalea, put it in a bright but not sunny place that is about 65F. Keep soil evenly moist, and mist leaves occasionally. As flowers fade (in about four or five weeks), reduce watering and allow the plant to rest. When warm weather starts (usually in May), first cut the plant back somewhat (leave about six inches of stems), and put it out side on a porch or windowsill. Resume regular watering at this time; repot, and start a mild feeding program. In early September move the plants indoors to a cool place and increase heat and water as the months go by. Plants should start showing buds around Christmas.

Treat plants the same way the second year as the first, except use a larger pot the second year. Watch azaleas to be sure they are not attacked by red spider mites. If you see the webs of these pests or silver-streaked leaves, use proper preventatives.

Begonia (Christmas begonia)

A good begonia can be covered with hundreds of flowers, usually pink. Unlike azaleas, begonias are not easy plants to grow (particularly this type) because they have a tendency to be temperamental and dislike drafts and fluctuating temperatures. But they are certainly worth trying to carry over through the year.

The flowers will last for some weeks if the plant is kept in a cool place (65F). Begonias like moisture, so keep soil well watered. When flowers fade, cut back the plant to about six inches to keep it growing. Now put the plant in warmth and bright light; soon new shoots will start into growth. When the shoots are about three or four inches tall, cut them from the mother plant and put them into a starter mix in shallow trays or pots. Cover the trays or pots with a plastic bag to ensure good humidity. Once roots form and plantlets are growing, put each one into rich soil in a six-inch pot. Grow them at a warm window where there is some sun.

Now treat the begonia as you would a standard plant: good moisture, bright light, and even humidity, and within a few months your new Christmas begonia will be in full leaf for another season of flowers. Avoid fluctuating temperatures and drafts because they can cause a begonia to wane.

New additions to the begonia family include the magnificently colored *Rieger-elatior* types. These bloom over a very long period and more and more are being used as gift plants. They need average home temperatures, evenly moist soil, and are much easier to grow than the Christmas begonias. However, they do have a drawback. I have noticed that my plants

74

get quite spindly, so cutting them back after blooming is a good idea to keep them bushy and handsome. The *Rieger* begonias are available under various names. My plant is "Aphrodite Cherry Red." I got it in November and it bloomed on and off until May—an excellent plant.

Calceolaria (pocketbook plant)

This funny little plant goes under the common name pocketbook plant because the flowers look like puffy pouches. The plants are small, inexpensive, and loaded with bloom in their season. Unfortunately, they are annuals, which means they last only one season. To keep them as long as possible, give them coolness and shade, with even moisture at the roots.

I cannot say much more about calceolarias because they are not really outstanding plants and, as annuals, they bloom only once. I have included them here only because they do have lovely color for a few weeks and are frequently given as gifts.

Camellia

Not many people think of camellias as houseplants, but if you have a cool place for them, camellias add much beauty indoors. Small treelike types are being offered as gift plants, and they are highly desirable because of their evergreen glossy foliage and of course, their stellar flowers. A good place for camellias is an unheated sun porch or perhaps a bay window.

The plants do not need direct sun but rather bright light and allow soil to dry out between waterings. Use an acid-type soil for the plants and prune plants every spring to encourage fresh, vigorous growth. Repot every second year and feed with appropriate fertilizer every month during the growing season.

Camellias as mentioned do well in unheated areas and are splendid decorations as floor plants in living rooms and other areas. It's unusual to see one in the home, but they *can* be grown and without much trouble; coolness is the key to success here.

CALCEOLARIA

Campanula (bellflower plant)

This is a large group of plants from temperate and tropical parts of the world. They are becoming popular as a houseplant because they have several attributes that make them most appealing to grow. Campanulas bear blue flowers, rare in the flower world, and the star- or bell-shaped blooms are charming. The plants are bushy, and many are natural trailers, making them ideal for hanging containers.

Campanulas are not easy plants to cultivate indoors, but they are not impossible. Basically they need a cool temperature (about 50F) to thrive and a bright place except in winter when it is essential they get some sun. Water plants copiously, then allow them to dry out before watering again. Apply a liquid food about once a month during the growing period.

Most campanulas are for outdoors, but some do exceptionally well indoors; this is especially true of *C. elatines*, sold as *C. isophylla mayi*, and *C. flore plena*.

To keep your campanula as long as possible—years, in fact—trim it back and keep the plant as cool as possible in late fall and early winter. This procedure works quite well: Trim off errant stems and leaves and cut back to about eight inches. Place the plant in an unheated but not freezing place—such as a pantry or a garage—until early spring. Then return the plant to the home at a bright window and increase moisture. When the plant is resting, water it only enough to keep soil from being caked.

Capsicum annum (pepper plant)

This handsome small plant appears in winter in florist shops. The pretty green leaves and bright red pepperlike fruit make it a desirable addition to any home. A tropical shrub from South America, the pepper plant requires warmth (78F) and copious water to be at its best. Generally, the plant, an annual, will be good only for a single season, but it is a long season, lasting from October well into February. The berries or "peppers" are green first, turning red as the days shorten.

The peppers are edible but extremely hot. Although an annual, capsicum frequently lives over from year to year—and my own is in its second year. This is the procedure I followed:

In late winter I trimmed it back radically, gave it fresh soil, and then kept it in a cool place, watering the plant just enough to keep soil from caking. In spring, I increased the moisture, light and temperature (75F), and the plant sprouted fresh growth.

This is a handsome indoor plant, and there are many varieties available. NOTE: Do not confuse this plant with the related *Solanum pseudo-capsicum,* known as the Jerusalem cherry.

Chrysanthemum

Florists carry pots of chrysanthemums several times a year. They make perfect gifts because they are loaded with blooms and brighten a scene like no other plant can. When you get chrysanthemums, keep them moist and somewhat cool (60F). Use them any place in the house where there is space. Once flowers fade, find a place for the plants in the garden; cut back plants to about six inches, and let them grow in the garden— next year they will bloom again. If you do not have a garden, put plants on a porch or balcony to start a second crop of flowers. There are dozens of chrysanthemums in many colors, and all are fine houseplants.

Cineraria

Cinerarias (*Senecio cruentus*) are absolutely stunning plants, with dazzling purple and blue flowers. These are impressive gifts, but unfortunately cinerarias are not amenable house denizens. They like very cool temperatures (55F), with some bright light, and no matter how you treat them, within a few weeks they are gone. Because they are annuals, cinerarias cannot be grown over, so their indoor value is temporary.

I have on occasion grown cinerarias for about six weeks,

CINERARIA

but that was their limit. I had to flood them every morning and spray them with Malathion for mite protection (mites love cinerarias). I also kept the plants outdoors as much as possible to lengthen their bloom. Do not count on this plant for color for a long time, but while it is with you it is magnificent.

Citrus

Dwarf citrus trees make ideal gift plants. These tiny trees can be with you for years, growing into very large handsome plants. Citrus are especially attractive, with glossy green leaves and nice branching habits, and there are a great many to choose from. For the most part, citrus like a light sunny place with average home temperatures. They enjoy good air circulation, and ample humidity (about forty percent). Keep soil evenly moist all year, and frequently mist leaves with water to prevent red spider mites from developing. These pests have an affinity for citrus plants, so be alert and catch them before they get a foothold. If water misting does not help, use a miticide such as Dimite.

The Meyer Lemon (*C. limonia meyeri*) is very popular, and the variety Ponderosa is equally as good. *C. mitis*, the miniature orange, is another good selection, and the Otaheite orange (*C. taitensis*) is a handsome small plant. There is also a lime available, *C. aurantifolia*, a small tree of about thirty-six inches.

All of the citrus make excellent houseplants and will be with you for years if grown with reasonable care. Every year citrus need repotting in fresh soil, and during the growing season (spring and summer) give them feedings once every two weeks with a weak plant food such as 10-10-5.

Columnea

These are large hanging plants of the gesneriad family or in some cases upright growers. Foliage varies in size and color; some plants have button leaves, others large elliptical leaves. The plants produce handsome tubular flowers in orange or

COLUMNEA

yellow. Generally, most species are epiphytic (air plants) so use a loose potting medium such as equal parts of osmunda or fir bark and soil. Like their cousins, African violets, columneas need a rather sunny window in winter and a shady place in summer. Keep the potting medium evenly moist and good humidity will produce a good crop of flowers.

Of the many varieties offered the most popular as a gift plant or most often seen in florist shops is the Belgian hybrid with orange flowers, and this is a highly recommended plant. It is a robust plant in comparison with some of the lesser types.

Cypripedium (lady's slipper orchid)

These large showy orchids are truly remarkable houseplants because they bloom indoors with little light. However, they do have a few stringent requirements: a half-and-half soil of fir bark and soil and a short resting period after flowering. Otherwise they are easily grown, even by the novice. The flower is waxlike and comes in a variety of color combinations, some quite exotic, and the blooms last a long time, from six to eight weeks on the plant (this in itself makes it a very desirable indoor subject).

There are so many hybrids available I cannot suggest specific ones; most are perfectly acceptable and some stellar. Of course the larger the flower—some to seven inches—the more costly the plant, but fine medium-sized flowering types cost only $5 to $10. If you want a foolproof orchid indoors and receive this one, you will be well pleased. Repot every year, but do not feed.

Dipladenia (Mexican love vine)

This colorful trailer from Mexico is becoming a very popular plant and justly deserves its reputation. With glossy green oval leaves and magnificent tubular shell pink blooms, dipladenia (*D. amoena*) is tough to beat for color and beauty. It grows well in a bright but not too sunny place and thrives on average home temperatures. Keep soil on the very moist side for best results. Peak bloom season is in late summer, but the Mexican love vine really bears blooms almost six months a year, one flower following the other in rapid succession. Spray plants with water mist frequently, and apply a monthly plant food in spring and summer, but not at all the rest of the year.

Although the plant is relatively easy to grow, dipladenia does not do well (and in fact may die) if kept in intense sun. But as mentioned, bright light is absolutely necessary to encourage flowering. Mealybugs and red spider mites have a liking for this plant, so keep close observation of leaves and stems for these culprits, especially in warm weather.

Dipladenias grow so well indoors that within a year you will have a full lush plant. It is an easy matter to divide the plant and get two from one: Simply run a knife through the crown of the plant where there is a natural division (you can see this by looking down at the plant). With only one or two dipladenias, in time you will have several for yourself or friends as a gift.

Euphorbia pulcherrima (poinsettia)

This favorite Christmas plant is a sight to see in bloom, with its green leaves and colorful bracts. Once there was only a red variety, but today white, pink, and greenish yellow poinsettias are also available. The plants are beautiful, but they are also somewhat difficult to maintain at home. The key to success with poinsettias is coolness; they need temperatures of about 50–55F to prosper, which is not easily achieved in most homes.

Soil should be evenly moist, and plants require good light. (Sunlight is not necessary and can harm plants.) To keep your poinsettia all year, in early spring cut it back and put it outdoors on a porch or in the garden. When fall comes, return the plant to a window indoors and increase watering until Novem-

POINSETTIA

ber, when it can be grown somewhat dry. Keep the plant in a dark place at night (where no artificial light gets to it) to encourage blooming in winter.

Today poinsettias also come in dwarf form. The excellent Mikkelson seems to be more robust and bear more flowers than the standard plants. Also, they are more easily grown and last in color for months.

Euphorbia splendens (crown-of-thorns)

Because of its bright red flowers and handsome branching shape, the crown-of-thorns has become a popular gift plant. It richly deserves its recent renaissance. This is an excellent indoor plant, one that grows easily without too much fuss. It requires a sandy soil, good bright light, and can withstand untenable conditions if necessary, being able to grow in coolness or in warmth. Most plants received will be about twenty inches tall, but within a year or so can reach forty-eight inches. Plants respond to some feeding all year, about every other month, with a soluble plant food.

The crown-of-thorns grows into a treelike shape and needs judicious pruning now and then to make it look its best. True to its name, the crown-of-thorns does have thorns, which can prick the skin, so be careful when handling the plant. Although *E. splendens* is the true species, many smaller varieties or improved types have been developed recently, including *E. splendens* Bowerji and a recent variety with yellow flowers. All seem to be amenable houseplants that will be with you for some time, even with minimum care.

Gardenia (cape jasmine)

These waxy, green-leaved, bushy plants have an army of followers. Your objective will be to coax the plants to bear their scented and lovely small white flowers. Perseverance is more the watchword with gardenias than care. When buds show, start misting them with warm water, and keep misting them whenever you think about it. If you do not moisten the

85

buds in this manner, they either drop off or refuse to open.

When you get your gardenia, put it in a cool (60F) place where there is some sun. To be sure that potting soil is right—and this is *important*—use a soil of equal parts loam, sand, and peat moss. Give the plant bright light in summer and sun in winter, and be sure to keep humidity as high as possible. Feed with a fish fertilizer once a month in spring and summer, and soak the plant in a sink or pail of water once a month. If night temperature is above 70F or below 60F, buds may fail to open. In the first year with you the gardenia most likely will not have too many flowers, but it is capable of adjusting to new conditions after a period of time, so if you can pull it through the initial months, it generally will remain with you as a good houseplant.

Like citrus plants, gardenias are fine food for red spider mites, so inspect and eliminate insects immediately when you see evidence of them. The gardenia grows rapidly and soon becomes a somewhat large and beautiful plant that looks stunning in a white glazed tub. Ask for it by its botanical name, *Gardenia jasminoides*.

Hedera helix (ivy)

Years ago, ivy was a most popular gift plant. It is vivid green, grows lushly and was generally considered an easy plant to grow. Today, most people realize how difficult ivy can be to grow and further, it always seems to attract red spider. Still, with its drawbacks ivy is making a comeback as a popular indoor plant and so is included here.

Plants come in many varieties and leaf colors and some are incredibly handsome; many are very suitable to training as topiaries; indeed, they grow very satisfactorily in this way.

Grow the plants as cool as possible (55–65F) and keep soil evenly moist but never soggy. Frequently, mist leaves with tepid water to deter red spider mites and give ivy a fairly bright but not sunny place. Quite contrary to most suggestions for ivy growing, I keep my plants well trimmed back; pruning ivy occasionally keeps it handsome.

Hibiscus

These are large plants with wonderful flowers, and most varieties bloom in the dreary winter, when color is so needed at home. The lush and leafy shrubby plants need a large container and require buckets of water and your sunniest window to bear flowers. The new varieties are highly desirable and have good strength. These are essentially outdoor plants that can serve easily as indoor plants. Just remember to give hibiscus plenty of water.

Because of their size—some grow to five feet—hibiscus need plenty of room to grow; a living-room corner near a window is ideal. If the plants lose leaves a few times a year, do not panic. This seems to be a natural tendency, and they soon leaf out again. If your plant does not respond to indoor conditions, try pruning it judiciously: Take about three or four inches off tip growth to encourage new growth. This method has worked for my plants.

Keep foliage misted, especially on hot days, and try to provide good humidity, at least forty percent.

Hydrangea

Widely sold at Easter as pot plants hydrangeas have a flamboyant beauty and do well to accent a room. The gift plant is usually a variety of *H. macropylla*, a deciduous shrub with showy clusters of white, pink, or blue flowers. (The coloring of the pink and blue types is determined by the degree of soil acidity.)

To maintain your hydrangea as long as possible, keep the soil evenly moist at all times; these plants do not tolerate dryness. Provide adequate humidity, about thirty percent, some sun and most important, coolness, never more than 70F. When spring frost is over place the potted plant outdoors in a partially shaded area and when blooms have faded cut them off. Now prune back the shoots about halfway. Repot in rich fresh soil. Keep the plants well watered and fed through the summer.

HIBISCUS

In fall (before weather turns cold) return the potted hydrangea to a cool (45–50F) place indoors in a very shady location. Keep soil just moist enough so that stems do not wither. After Christmas start forcing the hydrangea into growth by putting it in warmer temperatures, say 55–60F and where it is somewhat sunny. When leaves are actively growing, more warmth and water can be given the plant.

Several named varieties of hydrangeas are available and all are lovely colorful plants for your indoor garden.

Kalanchoe

These small charmers have come a long way since I first grew them in 1958. Today kalanchoes are available in several varieties, from red to orange to even pink. But my heart still belongs to the fiery red types derived from *K. blossfeldiana.* (Many names are now used, including Jingle Bells.)

Kalanchoes need little care to prosper indoors, but they do have some requirements, none difficult. First see that they are potted in somewhat sandy soil, and keep it moist at all times. Give the plants bright light (sun is not necessary), and because leaves are so closely crowded together, keep an alert eye for insects that can prosper in close quarters. I take my plants to a sink and spray leaves to flush off any possible insect eggs.

Because kalanchoes bloom at Christmas, they are especially desirable, and if you cut away faded flowers in, say, February, the plants bear another crop of blooms in April, a definite bonus. By all means do not miss the wonderful world of kalanchoes; they are stellar indoor plants.

Orchid (cattleya)

Of the hundreds of orchids available for home growing, the most popular is the corsage flower called cattleya. Unfortunately, it is a difficult orchid to grow indoors, but it is not impossible. So much extensive hybridization has been done that these fine plants are available in almost every color except

CATTLEYA

blue or black and every size from two to ten inches in diameter.

Plants have strap leaves and bear one, sometimes two, crops of flowers a year. Because cattleyas bloom four times a year, depending upon the variety, you are liable to get this plant in any season. For sheer drama cattleyas are tough to beat: Their flowers are regal and last for four to six weeks if the plants are kept in a cool place.

The main consideration with cattleyas is how to cope with them after bloom is over. This is the crucial time. Follow this strict procedure: Remove faded flowers, and then water the plant only once every ten days for about three months or until you see new growth start. When you see the first tip of green, repot the plant, being careful not to break the growing point. Put the plant into fir bark, *never* in soil. Water the bark lightly until the plant has established itself, which generally takes a month or so, and then resume regular waterings twice a week or more. Make sure the cattleyas have plenty of sun and warmth during the day and a cool temperature at night.

Some cattleyas of mine have bloomed religiously for years. In fact, the first plant I ever grew was a cattleya—a white one, and a gift for my birthday, twenty years ago.

Another orchid making strong inroads as a gift plant is phalaenopsis. It is the plant with wide spatula leaves and arching wands carrying dozens of white or pink flowers, quite a spectacle in bloom. It is available in winter which makes it an ideal gift during the holiday season.

Pelargonium (geraniums)

These festive plants offer almost constant color if given full sun and grown in a rather cool place with frequent airing and no crowding at windows. The family is so vast that it is difficult to suggest specifically which kind of geranium to grow, but there is a choice of zonals, standard types, carefree types, dwarfs, Martha Washington varieties, and the scented-leaf geraniums.

Whichever you choose, grow geraniums in a slightly acid soil; this is one time it pays to take the time to test the soil in the pot with a soil-testing kit. An acid soil should be about 6.5 to 7.0. Water the plants freely and then allow them to dry out somewhat before watering again. Geraniums bloom best when potbound, so grow the plants in small pots. The Martha Washington and scented types rest somewhat in winter, so water them moderately then and do not feed. Feed all other types once a month when the plants are in active growth, which is most of the time in sunny conditions. Avoid over-watering geraniums and be sure humidity is not too high in the growing area. As with most gift plants, coolness is preferred to warmth, and geraniums prosper at 55F, although daytime temperatures can be somewhat higher.

There are many different varieties, but the plants most offered by florists are the Martha Washington varieties or the fine zonals. However, miniatures are becoming popular and appearing at many stores. In any case, the geranium family offers a lot of good growing for indoor gardeners.

Primula (primrose)

These are very pretty little plants that come in a wide array of bright colors to glorify any area. Unfortunately, for all their decorative use, they are plants that last only a short time. Yet because they do add such a bright note of color in their season they are widely seen. Further, they are inexpensive, making an ideal gift plant for the budget-minded.

The plants require a cool place (55F) at a sunny window to be at their best. The period of blooming will last for about two weeks. Keep the soil evenly moist and move plants around the house for color accent as you need them. Once their season of bloom is over, you must discard the plants.

P. malacoides, known as the fairy primrose (and its varieties), is the one most often sold by florists. This is about a twelve-inch plant with vivid colorful blooms. *P. obconica*, a winter blooming primrose, is sometimes seen too. This plant is larger, both in leaf and flower. (Warning: The leaves can cause a skin rash.)

Saintpaulia (African violet)

The popularity of these perennial favorites cannot be challenged. They are excellent flowering indoor plants that have stood the test of time, and today there are better varieties than ever before. It is difficult to beat the venerable African violets as long-lasting gift plants. Flowers come in single, double, or semidouble forms in colors of pink, blue, lavender, purple, or white.

Give African violets bright light in spring and summer, some sun in fall and winter, and always a good circulation of air. Water soil moderately to keep it slightly moist but never wet; apply only tepid water because cold water can cause spots on leaves. Bottom watering (filling the saucer with water) is often advised to ensure even moisture at the roots, but you can water from the top too, alternating the two methods. Be sure all African violets have perfect drainage and good humidity of forty to sixty percent. Dryness in the air causes leaf curl and bud drop.

Observe plants frequently to be sure insects do not attack plants; if they do, take standard precautionary methods as described in Chapter 4. Keep African violets groomed to perfection, and turn plants once every few months so growth is symmetrical. The rosette shape of the violet is one of its attributes; a lopsided plant is less handsome.

There does not seem to be any particular peak season of bloom. I have had violets blooming year round and others that flower only in the winter. Because the plants have been hybridized so extensively, bloom seasons are lost in history, but African violets do bloom profusely indoors. Without doubt, this group of plants is one of the outstanding gift and houseplants available.

Solanum pseudo-capsicum (Jerusalem cherry)

Because of its colorful appearance—green leaves and red berries—the Jerusalem cherry from the Madeira islands is fine indoor color, whether you buy it or receive it as a gift. It has small rounded fruit, usually orange, but sometimes red, and grows to about twenty-four inches. It makes an ideal houseplant because it is neither too large nor too small. The berries are not edible.

Give the plant a light sunny place where it is somewhat cool (70F), and keep the soil evenly moist. To maintain the plant as long as possible, in spring cut back old plants to about two to four inches and keep soil barely moist for a few weeks; then treat the Jerusalem cherry as a regular houseplant.

The Jerusalem cherries are fine indoor subjects, especially effective if you group two or three in one area for a concentrated color display. Trim and prune errant stems and leaves as desired; it will not harm the plant in any way.

Trichocereus spachianus (cactus)

Two types of cactus have appeared as gift plants, and both are superlative for indoor growing. *Trichocereus spachianus* is a tall and ribbed columnar plant covered with white spines. (Zygocactus, the other gift cactus, is discussed at the end of the chapter.) Trichocereus is a floor or display plant and thus must be given a prominent place in a room. It is most effective when used against a white wall, where it looks like living sculpture or a substitute for furniture. Use handsome cylindrical white or terra-cotta pots to show off the plant.

Grow this cactus as you would other plants: routine waterings during the summer, twice a week, and waterings once a week in fall and winter. In winter, if it is possible, move the plant to a cooler place (60F). Remember that although most cacti are desert plants and do lead a dry existence in nature, in a pot of soil requirements differ: They need water just as other plants do. Sunlight is fine; indeed, trichocereus requires it to stay in good health.

Insects rarely invade cacti. The only potential problem is crown rot if you overwater the plant. To avoid crown rot, put a layer of white gravel over the top of the soil to protect the crown of the plant from excessive water. Cacti grow slowly and will be with you for years, so as gift plants they are really worth the money.

Zygocactus (Christmas, Easter, Thanksgiving Cacti)

The Christmas cactus, Easter cactus, and Thanksgiving cactus have an array of botanical names, including Zygocactus (Christmas or Thanksgiving), Schlumbergera (Easter), and Rhipsalidopsis (Christmas or Easter). I discovered that my so-called Christmas cactus was a Thanksgiving one, and my Easter cactus was really a Christmas one. So do not worry about the botanical names of these plants.

Zygocacti are low-growing, somewhat pendant plants, with flowers borne on the tips of the leaves. The green leaves are scalloped, resembling a crab's claw. Colors vary from pink to almost brick red, and a well-grown plant can be covered with a halo of color. Zygocactus require some stringent but not impossible conditions to thrive.

Unlike most cactus that grow in the desert, these gift ones naturally grow in shady and moist rain forests. Zygocacti are epiphytes (air plants) which means that they like a good circulation of air, shade, and ample moisture. It also means that these plants need a somewhat different soil mix than most plants. Air plants do not like their roots smothered in tight soil; they prefer a mixture of fir bark and soil.

Zygocactus require good moisture, bright light, and average home temperatures in the home all year. To make your cactus bloom, in September put it in a dark place where natural light cannot get to it; any artificial light whatsoever will inhibit or completely curtail bud formation. Keep the plant there for six to eight weeks and do water it. Once buds show, move the plant to any area for bloom. If you have an Easter cactus, start the dark inhibition period six to eight weeks prior to Easter; start a Thanksgiving cactus six to eight weeks before

CHRISTMAS CACTUS

that holiday. Normally these plants are rarely bothered by pests of any type, respond well to routine culture, and need only darkness to bloom.

SEE GIFT PLANT CHART ON FOLLOWING PAGE

Gift Plant Chart

BOTANICAL AND COMMON NAME	LIGHT	TEMPERATURE	WATER*	REMARKS
Aechmea chantini	Bright	70–80F	EM	Large but beautiful
A. fasciata (Grecian urn plant)	Bright	70—80F	EM	Stellar plant
Aesychynanthus speciosa (lipstick vine)	Sun	75–80F	Allow to dry between waterings	Excellent color
Amaryllis	Sun	70—80F	EM	Always dependable
Anthurium (flamingo flower)	Bright	75–85F	EM	Blooms last a long time

Plant	Light	Temperature		Notes
Azalea	Bright	55–65F	AM	Stellar color
Begonia (Christmas begonia)	Bright	50–60F	AM	Difficult
B. Rieger-elatior	Sun	55–65F	AM	Good new introduction
Calceolaria (pocketbook plant)	Sun	60–80F	AM	Easy
Camellia	Bright	50—55F	Keep soil evenly moist	Difficult but not impossible
Campanula (bellflower)	Bright	50–65F	EM	Worth the trouble
Capsicum annuum (pepper plant)	Bright	55–60F	EM	Always dependable

Gift Plant Chart

Cattleya	Sun	60–75F	Allow to dry between waterings	Allow to rest
Chrysanthemum	Sun	60–80F	AM	Must have sun
Cineraria	Bright	60–70F	AM	Good seasonal plant
Citrus: Meyer Ponderosa Mitis Otaheite	Bright	60–80F	Water; allow to dry out before watering again	Excellent trees
Columnea (Belgian hybrids)	Bright	70–80F	AM	Orange flowers

Plant	Light	Temperature		Notes
Cypripedium (lady's slipper orchid)	Bright	65–75F	EM	Blooms last long time
Dipladenia amoena (Mexican love vine)	Sun	70–80F	EM	Fine for beginner
Euphorbia pulcherrima (poinsettia)	Bright	55–65F	AM	Fine new varieties
E. splendens (crown-of-thorns)	Sun	55–75F	EM	Good branching plant
Gardenia jasminoides (cape jasmine)	Sun	65–75F	EM	Tricky, but not impossible
Hedera helix (ivy)	Bright	55–65F	EM	Can attract insects
Hibiscus	Sun	75-85F	Dry	Stellar plant

Gift Plant Chart

Hydrangea	Bright	50–60F	EM	Very colorful
Kalanchoe	Bright	70–80F	Dry out	Excellent and easy
K. "Jingle Bells"	Bright	70–80F	Dry out	Bright red flowers
K. "Tom Thumb"	Bright	70–80F	Dry out	Small charmer
Phalaenopsis (moth orchid)	Bright	70–80F	Dry out	Good indoor orchid
Pelargonium (geranium)	Bright	55–65F	Dry out	Likes coolness
Primula (primrose)	Sun	65–75F	EM	Short-lived

Saintpaulia (African violet)	Shade	70–80F	EM	Favorite plant
Solanum pseudo-capsicum (Jerusalem cherry)	Shade	65–75F	EM	Unusual
Trichocereus spachianus (cactus)	Bright	65–80F	Dry	Can't kill
Zygocactus (Christmas cactus)	Bright	65–75F	EM	Real beauty

*EM = evenly moist; AM = almost moist (dry to the touch)

8
Flowering Bulbs

This section is included because recently many florists have been offering some of the more unusual bulbs as gift plants. Besides the familiar crocus—veltheimia, eucharis, eucomis, and haemanthus (the blood lily)—are splendid indoor additions that will live for years with suitable care. This is what this chapter is all about: How to care for bulbs properly.

Hints on Bulbs

Most of the bulbs described here are tender ones that can be carried over year to year. They grow most of the year, with a slight rest period in the winter. Some (in pots) must be put away (in a brown bag) for a few months in a cool dark area to regain vigor and get ready for next year's flowers, but others grow on all year.

The secret about growing bulbs is to start them into growth slowly. If you receive the bulb rather than a mature plant, give it moderate waterings, and increase moisture as leaves start to grow. Feedings once every two weeks with a mild plant food (10-10-5) and a pinch of bone meal ensure healthy plants. Use a rich soil; drainage is vital for bulbs.

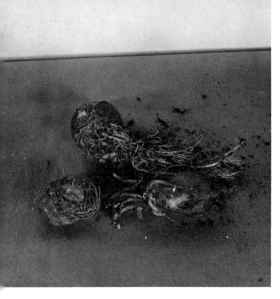

Bulbs of many plants are available at suppliers in seasonal times, ready for planting and cultivation. *(Photo by Matthew Barr)*

(When I talk about bulbs in this book I use it as an all inclusive term for corms, rhizomes, pips, and tubers.)

Bulbous plants are now being offered as gifts in kits with planting mix and containers (amaryllis, for example). (I think we will see more packaged bulbs in the near future.) Or you may receive mature plants grown from bulbs already in bloom. With these plants follow this procedure: Grow them until flowering is over; then taper off watering so they can rest for about six weeks. Some will have to be stored (pot and all) in a cool but not freezing place such as a garage or pantry. Other bulbous plants (and these are mentioned in plant descriptions) grow all year.

Most people are somewhat confused about which end of a bulb goes into the planting mix and how far it should be imbedded. Look at the bulb; most are tapered, and the tip end is the end that protrudes above the soil line. Generally, but not always, the soil should reach the collar of the plant; it should never be above this area or rot may develop.

A compendium of some fine gift bulb plants—and how to grow them—follows.

106

AMARYLLIS

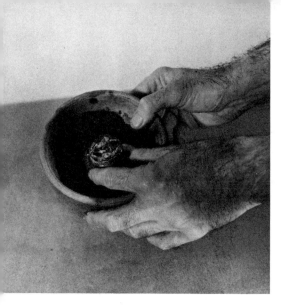

An amaryllis bulb is planted in rich soil; note that the bulb is not buried deeply. *(Photo by Matthew Barr)*

Amaryllis

These incredible plants, long-time favorites, are excellent gifts. The flowers, some seven inches across, are the main attraction and come in white, red, pink, rose, and violet, with red being the most popular color. Bulbs or plants in flower are available (at seasonal times) from January to March. If you get a bulb use one to a six- or seven-inch pot, allowing one inch of space between the walls and the bulb. Do not bury the bulb; allow the upper third to stay above the soil line. Moisten the soil, and set the pot in a cool shady place. Grow the plant just barely moist until the flower stalk (which comes before the leaves) is about eight inches tall. Then move the plant into a sunny place and water heavily. Amaryllis take about one month to bear their magnificent flowers.

After the plants bloom, keep the foliage growing so the leaves can manufacture food for next year's flowers. Do not throw the bulb away when foliage turns brown; keep it in a cool shady place with the soil almost dry for about three months or until you see new growth starting. Then replant the amaryllis in fresh soil (use the same container; amaryllis like small pots). If you can, put the plant outdoors to benefit from

The amaryllis in full flower.
(Photo by author)

fresh rains and warmth; otherwise keep it at a sunny window. In fall the amaryllis should have cool temperatures (60F). Increase watering and wait for the next cycle of blooms.

There are many named varieties of amaryllis, but generally they are sold by color rather than by name.

Crinum

This excellent amaryllis produces lilylike pink or red flowers from April to summer. *C. moorei, C. giganteum,* and *C.* "Ellen Bousanquet" are ideal crinums to try. Plant one bulb per ten-inch pot in a rich, sphagnum-containing soil. Leave half the bulb above the surface. Good drainage is essential, so put gravel at the bottom of the pot. Start plants in late fall. Water slightly until growth starts, at which point increase moisture and start feeding once every two weeks. Give plants bright light but never intense sun. Plants can be rested and started again each year, but they can also be grown all year. Repot every four years.

Crocus

These favorite flowers, so associated with early spring, are featured at florists in season. You can buy the plants already in bloom or plant the corms and start your own which is much more fun. Put six to eight of the small bulbs in a five- or six-inch pot filled with gravel or sandy soil. Water moderately until growth shows and leave in bright light; move to better light at this time. Flowers last from several days to a few weeks but after blooming the bulbs must be discarded. Still, while they are in color they are worthwhile additions to the indoor garden.

Colchicum autumnale, also called crocus, grows from a corm rather than a bulb and blooms in fall. They are so easy to grow that they are sometimes called "magic plants," for they can bloom even out of soil!

Cyclamen

These plants, which grow from a corm, appear in florist shops in February or March. They are low-growing plants with rich green leaves and nodding flowers in white, pink, or red on medium to tall stems. The plants add great glamour to a room and are small; thus they can be used in many areas indoors. Healthy plants will bear flowers for a period of several weeks, one following the other in a gay procession of color. When you receive a cyclamen, put it in a cool place and drench it daily—this plant loves water.

When blooms fade, let the plant die back, and reduce moisture and temperature. If weather is good, plunge the pot into the ground outside in a shady place and forget it for a while. In June or July check to see if new growth has started. If it has, start watering the plant heavily. In September take the

CYCLAMEN

**A favorite gift plant grown from a corm is the cyclamen.
The new varieties are very robust.** *(Photo by Matthew Barr)*

plant from the garden, place it at a sunny window, and continue watering and feeding.

Another way to keep cyclamens over (and one I did suc-
cessfully in my Chicago apartment) is to remove the corms
from the soil after the bloom time. Put them in brown bags
and store them in a cabinet in an unheated but not freezing
pantry. Let them rest for several months; start them in fresh
soil about May. When you restart cyclamens this way, give
them little water for the first few weeks, increasing moisture
as growth increases. Always keep cyclamens out of the sun.
These are really excellent little plants that can, without too
much trouble, be carried over for several years.

Eucharis (Amazon lily)

This is one of my favorites, and you should try it because it is impossible to fail with this bulb. The Amazon lily bears fragrant white flowers on twelve-inch stems; generally in spring or summer (do *not* cut flowers), but mine also bloomed once in the winter. Cover bulbs about half their depth with coarse fibrous soil. Water sparingly until growth starts, but always keep soil somewhat moist. Keep warm temperatures of 70–80F to encourage the bulbs to sprout. Make sure plants have good sun all year. During the plant's resting period, decrease waterings and the temperature to 60F. Do not remove bulb from pot but move to a cool place as mentioned and keep soil barely moist. In a few months repot in fresh soil, move to warmth and increase waterings. *E. grandiflora* is the species most offered.

Eucomis (pineapple lily)

This exquisite flowering plant thrives indoors in a pot; it has dozens of tiny whitish green flowers and bright green leaves resembling pineapple foliage, thus the plant's common name. The best species for indoors are *E. undulata* and *E. punctata.*

In the fall, plant bulbs with the crown about one inch deep in a sandy soil. Barely water until February; then increase watering. Keep plants in shade until leaves start growing. Plants can then be moved into light. Maintain a night temperature of 50F, and grow the plant in the same ten- or twelve-inch tub for several years without repotting. Decrease moisture somewhat in winter but never allow the soil to become bone dry.

Gloriosa (glory lily)

This tropical lily has exotic red and yellow flowers and although I have seen these for sale as mature plants, you may receive tubers. In the fall, plant one tuber just below the surface of a sandy soil in an eight-inch pot and water moderately until leaves show. Maintain a warm temperature of 75F, with

113

Here cyclamens are used in a planter to decorate a room with a fine splash of color. *(Photo by Max Eckert)*

bright but not sunny light. Once leaves are four or five inches tall water more often. After flowers fade allow foliage to turn yellow; then store tubers in a cool dark place for three or four months. Start them into growth again in fresh soil.

If you receive a mature plant simply grow-on as explained above. *G. rothschildiana* is the most popular species.

Hamaenthus (Blood lily)

This is a spring- or fall-flowering amaryllis from South Africa with one hundred or more tiny, exquisite flowers to a crown. Bulbs are large, so use only one in an eight-inch pot. Plant firmly in a rich, fast-draining soil. Leave the top one-half inch of the bulb protruding. Start bulbs in fall with little watering. After growth appears, water copiously and feed the blood lily every other week with a weak liquid fertilizer. These plants cannot take summer sun, so shade them. In the other seasons sun will not harm hamaenthus.

There are three outstanding types of blood lily. *H. katherinae*, which blooms in spring after foliage ripens, is a beautiful red. This evergreen plant does not have to be stored away. *H. multiflorus* generally blooms first, and then sprouts foliage. This lily lies dormant in the winter. *H. coccineus* grows all winter but is dormant in summer. *H. multiflorus* and *H. coccineus* need a resting period: Barely water them, lower temperatures to 50F, and make sure plants are in total darkness.

Hyacinth

You have probably noticed hyacinths in glass vases at florists. These plants are frequently grown in water alone or water and pebbles and bloom with little care. For pot culture use a four- or five-inch container with sandy soil; there are hyacinths for early bloom, midseason and late color. You can have a succession of fragrant flowers for many months if you stagger plantings.

Narcissus are favorite bulbous plants and add beauty to a room. Here they bloom profusely in a shallow bowl of pebbles. *(Photo by Roche)*

Constant moisture is necessary for hyacinths and good bright light. As with most bulbs, start in coolness (55–60F) and filtered light and as growth progresses move to warmth and more light. Not overly dramatic, hyacinths are worthwhile for fragrance as well as color.

Narcissus

Narcissus, sometimes called paper-whites or daffodils, are favorite bulbs that bear white or yellow flowers, usually sweetly scented. Bulbs are started, six or eight to a six-inch container, in pebbles, and are good only for the season. Keep the gravel moist at all times and until the plants have made foliage growth leave them in a shady place. Then they can be placed at a bright window. You can buy bulbs and start them or you may receive blooming plants. In either case, once flowering is over they must be discarded.

Miniature daffodils can also be grown indoors in pots of gravel for seasonal color. *(Photo courtesy Burpee Seed Co.)*

Ornithogalums are frequently overlooked bulbous plants and they do make pretty gift plants grown in pots. *(Photo courtesy Wayside Gardens)*

Ornithogalum

Ornithogalums are especially good for cut flower arrangements (see also Chapter 10). White or yellow flowers develop from a leafless stalk. The three most readily available species are *O. arabicum*, which has white flowers with a greenish eye, *O. thyrsoides*, which has white flowers with a brown center, and *O. aureum*, which has yellow flowers. Grow these flowering bulbs in a window garden for attractive accent in the dreary winter months.

Plant six or seven bulbs to an eight-inch pot between September and November. Maintain cool temperatures until growth starts, and then increase moisture, warmth, and light. Ornithogalums need plenty of water. When flowers fade, let the bulbs dry off gradually. Keep bulbs in the same pots and rest them in 55F temperature until September or November.

Oxalis

Considered weeds outdoors, indoors oxalis yields white, yellow, or red flowers that usually bloom on and off all year.

118

O. bowieana has red flowers, *O. cernua* has flamboyant bright yellow flowers, *O. hirta* bears rose-pink flowers, and *O. rubra* has veined rose blooms. All are good varieties for your indoor display. Summer and fall varieties need a winter resting period. In the fall, push three or four corms about two inches below the soil line in an eight-inch pot. Keep soil barely wet until growth starts; then increase watering. Feed plants twice a month with a fertilizer that contains some bone meal. Ample sunlight will produce an abundance of flowers.

Sinningia (gloxinia)

These glamorous plants from tropical Brazil go under the botanical name Sinningia. Plants have single or double tubular or slipper-shaped flowers in vivid colors. Hybrids that bloom at various times through the year have been developed, so you can expect this plant as a gift almost any time.

Plants will be in bud or flower when you receive them. The cooler and shadier you keep them, the longer they will last. When you notice flowers fading, reduce watering. Remove tops and store bulbs in a cool shady place. Keep soil barely moist, and let the bulbs rest for about eight weeks. Then repot in fresh soil in a larger pot (one to a pot): Set the bulbs with the hollow side up, and cover with soil. Keep the soil evenly moist, at about 60F. Increase water and warmth when growth starts to flourish, and then get ready for more flowers.

There are many magnificent hybrids, some with mammoth flowers, and these rather than the smaller species are the ones used as gift plants. Gloxinias make fine accents on tables or desks where some color is needed.

Vallota (Scarborough lily)

This South African evergreen bulb has dazzling red flowers, in spring or summer, on ten-inch stems. Vallota bulbs are expensive but worth it; use *V. speciosa*. Plants like to be crowded so use the smallest pot you can. Plant the bulb with its nose

GLOXINIA

slightly above the soil line. Use a rich, well-draining soil (one-half inch of gravel in the bottom of the pot will ensure good drainage). Keep plants in a bright but not sunny place, water moderately, and feed every two weeks. Repot only when absolutely necessary. Vallotas are slow growing, so do not be surprised if the plant does not bloom the first year.

Veltheimia

This plant from the Cape of Good Hope has pendant yellow flowers tinged red. *V. viridifolia* is the popular species. Start bulbs in late fall, one to a pot, in loose soil. Plants must have good drainage and fairly dry soil until growth starts. Once growth begins, heavily water the plant through the growing cycle. Feed plant every two weeks, grow in full sun, and maintain a 55F temperature. Once the flowers fade, let the leaves turn yellow. Then stop watering. Store the bulb in its pot for about two months. Repot in the fall in fresh soil.

Flowering Bulbs Plant List

BOTANICAL AND COMMON NAME	LIGHT	TEMPERATURE	WATER*	REMARKS
Amaryllis	Bright	60–70F	EM	Stellar flowers
Crocus	Bright	55–65F	EM	Colorful accent
Cyclamen	Shade	55–65F	AM	Robust plants
Crinum	Sun	60–70F	AM	Unusual
Eucharis (Amazon lily)	Bright	60–70F	EM	Foolproof
Eucomis (pineapple lily)	Sun	60–70F	EM	Overlooked beauty
Gloriosa (glory lily)	Sun	70–80F	AM	A favorite

Plant	Light	Temperature	Moisture	Notes
Hamaenthus (blood lily)	Bright	70–80F	EM	Stellar plant
Hyacinth	Bright	55–65F	EM	Get indoor types
Narcissus (daffodil)	Bright	60–75F	AM	Easy
Ornithagalum	Sun	60–70F	AM	Good cut flowers
Oxalis	Sun	70–80F	AM	Bloom profusely
Sinningia (gloxinia)	Shade	55–65F	AM	Many kinds
Vallota (Scarborough lily)	Bright	60–70F	EM	Stellar plant
Veltheimia	Bright	65–75F	EM	Unusual plant

*EM = evenly moist; AM = almost moist (dry to the touch)

9

Gift Plant Arrangements

Gift plants can also include such popular items as dish gardens, terrariums, and plants in hanging baskets. Care of these items involves some simple tricks to get the most from them. Some of these gifts, notably the terrarium and dish garden, can be quite expensive, so of course you will want to keep them as long as possible. And there is no reason why a beautiful terrarium brimming with plants should not last a whole year. Trailing plants in hanging containers are also favorites, and many require specific hanging equipment and special saucers for catching excess water.

Dish Gardens

I can remember my grandmother making these diminuitive landscaped arrangements of plants in a dish. Later I made dish gardens of my own, advancing to very elaborate ones, minute to every detail, based on research I did for a book I wrote about dish gardens. The dish garden you receive will most likely be a Christmas present because this is the season of their greatest popularity. The dishes are inexpensive and plain, but very satisfactory. Unlike the florists' dish gardens of my teenage years, those available today can be works of

125

Here the author makes a dish garden to give to a friend. A standard clay pot is used, and small plants are best. *(Photo by Matthew Barr)*

art, with every detail finely and delightfully executed. There is very little you have to do to maintain them. Put the garden in a bright but not sunny place, water it about twice a week, and sit back and enjoy the little scene. Usually within a year or so the plants will outgrow the garden (unless they are true miniatures), so you will have to redo the lilliputian scene. But the plants you remove can be repotted easily and used as window plants.

On the other hand, some dish gardens may not be as well designed as others, but merely a collection of plants. To some this note of greenery is fine, but most people will want to rearrange the plants and create their own dish garden. What you want are true miniatures in a simulated, eye-pleasing scene. This means that you might have to do some landscaping. Keep little-leaved plants intact, but remove large growers.

126

Make a contoured landscape that resembles some natural scene by creating hills and valleys, never a straight terrain. Embed small rocks and interesting pieces of wood into the soil. Use gravel and colored sand to create paths and walks or hilly ledges. Make it natural. Use small slow-growing plants, or try some of the fine miniature African violets or begonias for a really super garden.

Use what you want and discard what you do not want until the total scene is pleasing. This might involve spending extra money for a few plants, but the cost is worth it because a well-done dish garden is beautiful (I had some that lasted four and five years): simple scenes in simple containers and magnificent accents for a small living-room table or desk. See list at end of next section for plants.

The completed dish garden; some rocks will be added in the foreground. *(Photo by Matthew Barr)*

A handsome dish garden with mistletoe, fig, and selaginella. *(Photo by Clark Photo Graphics)*

Terrariums

The renaissance of the terrarium has been most satisfying. When I wrote my first book on terrariums in 1968, I had to use discarded jars and jugs for containers since nothing else was available. By the time I wrote my second terrarium book (1973), countless containers and kits were being sold. Terrariums have come a long way, for a definite reason: Once set up properly, with all elements balanced, the enclosed greenery can operate on its own with little help from you. Condensation on the glass creates moisture that rolls down into the soil to water the plants. This process continues indefinitely, leaving you free to just sit back and enjoy the terrarium.

The only secret to creating a terrarium is balancing all the elements. There must be enough space in the terrarium for the plants, air, soil, light, and the balanced environment is thus created. Some terrariums from florists may have been done properly with these factors in mind, in which case no remaking or arranging is needed. Others—the majority, I am sorry to say—leave a great deal to be desired; you will have to do some rearranging. But this is easy.

First, any terrarium you get that has less than three gallons capacity is bound to be a difficult project to handle. I have, after much experience, been able to balance a standard wine-bottle terrarium, but it was difficult, and the terrarium did not last more than six months. (A terrarium should last for years.)

If the terrarium you receive is crowded, remove some plants and reestablish the terrain. The soil should be rather hilly, never level. Embed stones and make rock cliffs to simulate a natural scene. Use small plants like peperomias and pilea or true miniatures if you can find them. And again, *balance* the scene. If daily condensation is so heavy that it is impossible to see the plants inside, the balance is off. Remove some plants. Some moisture should gather on the inside of the glass, but mainly at night. It should be gone by early morning. So it is necessary to observe terrariums.

At attractive terrarium made in a ginger jar; note the arc arrangement of the plants and the ground cover used to clothe soil. *(Photo by Matthew Barr)*

A well-grown terrarium in a plastic container; such small gardens make handsome accents on tables and are ideal as gifts. *(Photo by Matthew Barr)*

Good plants for the terrarium and dish garden:

Acorus gramineus pusillus (sweet flag). Excellent bottle plant. Tuftlike grassy leaves, two to three inches high.

Aechmea racinae. Ten-inch bromeliad with shiny dark green straplike leaves and a rosette shape.

Aglaonema pictum (Chinese evergreen). One of the best foliage plants with blue-green leaves splashed with silver. Somewhat large, but can be trimmed to desired shape and size.

Alternanthera bettzickiana. This bright miniature has yellow, pink, red, and green foliage. Group a few of these in one area for some concentrated color.

Anthurium scherzerianum (flamingo plant). Attractive green leaves and red shiny bracts.

Bambusa nana (bamboo). Grassy plant that needs severe pruning; use only a few shoots.

130

Calathea bachemiana. Not really a miniature, but a lush plant with velvety gray-green leaves edged with dark green. Also handsome is *C. picturata argentea,* with silver leaves etched in dark green.

Chamaeranthemum igneum. This tropical creeper has velvety bronze-brown leaves and pink veins.

Crassula cooperi. This is a three-inch leathery leaved plant. *C. schmidtii* is also handsome, with its red-tinted leaves. Many other small species are available.

Cryptanthus bromelioides tricolor. One of the best small bromeliads, with rosettes of green leaves striped pink and white. *C. bivittatus (roseus picta)* has bronze-pink foliage striped pale green, *C. acaulis* has bronze-green foliage, *C. terminalis* has bronze-green foliage and *C. beuckerii* has pale green foliage.

Dracaena godseffiana. This is a slow-growing yellow- and green-leaved plant. Prune to keep small.

Drosera rotundifolia. Tiny insect eater; spoon-shaped growth covered with red hairs tipped in a sticky substance. Insect landing on plant is trapped and pulled into plant.

Ficus radicans variegata. Dainty foliage creepers, with silver-green leaves marked white. Also desirable is *F. repens pumila,* with heart-shaped dark green foliage. It sends out disks that cling to glass.

Fittonia verschaffeltii (mosaic plant). This slow-growing creeper has iridescent foliage. Will remain dwarf size.

Haworthia limifolia. Small succulent with ribbed leaves.

Hedera helix. Large group of delightful ivies; many well suited for the glass garden.

Helxine soleirolii (baby's tears). One of the most refreshing wee creepers around, with buttonlike bright green leaves. Rampant grower; use sparingly.

Malpighia coccigera (miniature holly). Glossy green leaves and pink flowers. Robust.

Maranta oppenheimiana tricolor. This stellar foliage plant has flowing multicolored foliage. Also try *M. leucuheura kerchovena.*

Pelliona repens. This small creeper has elliptical metal-green foliage. Plant will stay small.

Peperomia. A group of many miniatures, most with heart-shaped or oval leaves. Try "Little Fantasy" with silver-green and brown leaves; "Pixie" with bright green leaves; *P. rubella* with moss green foliage; and *P. obtusifolia* with variegated foliage.

Pilea. A genus of fleshy creepers. *P. cadierei minima* (aluminum plant) has silver-green foliage; *P. depressa* has sea-green toothed leaves; *P. nunmulariaefolia* has heart-shaped fuzzy green leaves; *P. repens* has tiny, round, bronze foliage; and *P. microphylla* is a tiny-leafed beauty.

Selaginella kraussiana brownii. This is a creeping, grass-green, mossy plant. *S. uncinata* is another fine one, with tiny blue-green leaves.

Inspect your new glass garden every day the first few weeks to be sure all the elements are in balance. If they are not, correct the balance. Create your own favorite scene; use proper plants and enjoy your gift. The original giver will never notice a good rearrangement. In most cases he or she will be amazed to see the terrarium still alive and growing even years later.

132

A large hanging fern used as a basket plant decorates the author's plant room. Ferns are popular gift plants and also make fine garden-in-the-air accents. *(Photo by Matthew Barr)*

Hanging Gardens

Trailing plants hung at eye level are infinitely handsome. This is an ideal way to grow most trailing plants because they can enjoy good light and air. Plants most often used in hanging containers are Swedish ivy, cissus (kangaroo ivy), chlorophytum (spider plant), and various tradescantias and zebrinas, which are natural trailers.

133

The main consideration with your gift hanging garden is where to put it. Logically the most ideal spot is near a window, which is fine. But do not suspend the plant so that it is too high, or so low that it impedes traffic. Place the plant properly to get the most out of it, and remember that it must be within your reach so you can water it—removing plants and taking them to the sink for watering is really a chore.

Hang your plant your height plus the height of a long-necked watering can. Hang it with stout chain; a hanging plant can weigh twenty to thirty pounds, and I have seen too many plants fall from string or wire moorings. Suspend the chain from an eye or an S hook, and be sure it is really in the ceiling; that is, it should be screwed into a ceiling joist so it is in contact with wood and thus able to hold the weight of the plant. If the hook is just stuck in plaster, it will invariably loosen and drop with quite a jar to both you and the plant. Most ceiling joists are on sixteen- or eighteen-inch centers, so this should give you a clue as to where you will find a solid piece of wood to use as a mooring.

A trailing columnea on a plastic stand makes an extraordinary decorative accent. *(Photo by Clark Photo Graphics)*

Once your plant is in place, be sure it is level and has some device attached underneath—a saucer or pan clipped on to the pot—to catch the excess water. Otherwise the floor will get the brunt of the water and in time become stained. Nurseries and florists sell suitable hanging saucers and drip catchers. A deep hook-on dish is my favorite.

Most hanging plants can take good light and, in fact, should have ample light and some sun if possible. Use the brightest place in your apartment or home for a hanging plant. Water routinely, twice a week, and enjoy your hanging garden. By the way, one plant always looks a little awkward and lonely. Try a couple for a real display.

Good plants for hanging gardens

Asparagus sprengeri (asparagus fern). Charming plant with arching fronds of needlelike leaves. Easy to grow.

Abutilon hybridum (flowering maple). Maplelike leaves and bell-shaped orange flowers. Beautiful but tends to get straggly. Cut back every few months.

Beloperone guttata (shrimp plant). Deep green leaves and coral-colored bracts. Somewhat temperamental.

Bougainvillea. Paper thin leaves and lovely red bracts. Will grow indoors if enough sun.

Browallia speciosa. Really an outdoor plant but will grow indoors too. A bounty of white-throated violet flowers.

Campanula. Blue flowers and small green leaves. Many varieties.

Chlorophytum elatum (spider plant). Graceful grassy leaves in rosettes. Grows like a weed and pretty.

Cissus antarctica (kangaroo ivy). Large-toothed dark green leaves. Fast grower.

C. rhombifolia (grape ivy). Glossy-toothed and pointed leaves. Fast growing.

Clerodendrum thompsoniae. Lovely green leaves and pure white and red flowers. Big but beautiful.

Coleus. Often sold; colorful foliage but difficult plant to grow. Needs buckets of water to thrive.

Dipladenia amoena (Mexican love vine). Crinkled green leaves and rose pink flowers. A charmer.

Ferns. Many varieties; most make excellent hanging plants; lush green fronds, rosette growth.

Ficus pumila (creeping fig). Tiny button leaves; dense ball of color and easy to grow.

Gynura aurantiaca (velvet plant). Purple leaves, scandent growth. Tough one to cultivate.

Hedera helix (English ivy). Small dark green scalloped leaves; a favorite plant but difficult to grow well. Subject to red spider mites attack.

Hoya carnosa (wax plant). Small gray-green oval leaves; only mature plants bloom. Fine house plant.

Impatiens. Dark green leaves and scarlet blooms. Not really a trailer but makes lovely halo of color. Ask for Elfin varieties.

Petunia. Beautiful flowering plants that need no description. Ask for cascading varieties. Can't miss with these. Good for one season only.

Ruellia makoyana. Silver-veined leaves and red flowers. An overlooked plant and a good one.

Saxifraga sarmentosa (strawberry geranium). Small soft, round hairy leaves. Charming.

Scindapsus aureus (ivy arum). Very popular with heart-shaped dark green leaves marked yellow. Needs plenty of water.

Tolmiea menziesii (piggyback plant). Rosette growth; somewhat fuzzy scalloped green leaves. Difficult to grow.

Zebrina, Tradescantia (wandering Jew). Two types here, one with green leaves, others green with pink or white stripes. Many varieties. All good.

10
Gift Plant Bonus

Most of the plants you receive will be mature and after a few months may be large enough to divide into two plants. Or, as is the case with bromeliads and orchids, they may throw offshoots that can be removed and potted for a new plant. Other plants can be propagated from leaf or stem cuttings to get bonus plants that will cost you almost nothing.

Aside from a container and soil, the bonus plant is a dividend from nature, so there is no sense in not using it wisely. Besides, everyone likes something for nothing, and many of the gift plants are more than generous with offspring.

Basic Care of Plantlets

Some simple general-care rules apply to all young plants. The time involved is minimal, based on the following procedure:

1. Put cuttings, leaves, offshoots, or divisions into a shallow container that is about four to six inches deep. Use a starter mix, and fill the container to within one inch of the rim of the container. Moisten the medium and insert the plantlet.

139

Gift plants like chlorophytum have many hanging plantlets which can be cut and rooted to provide new plants. *(Photo by author)*

2. Water thoroughly with a fine mist, and place the container in a warm (78F) and bright but not sunny light. To ensure good humidity, which is essential to get plants growing, put sticks in each corner of the container and plastic over the sticks to form a tent. If too much moisture accumulates on the inside of the tent, remove the plastic for a few hours.

3. In a few weeks, remove the plastic (remember always to keep the medium uniformly moist—too much water will cause rot, and not enough water may cause the plant to die). Move the container to a brighter place.

4. In another few weeks, remove plantlets and see if roots have formed. If so, pot plantlets individually in soil. If roots have not formed, return the plantlets to the medium.

Containers

Containers for starting your new plants can be anything, from aluminum pans for frozen rolls or cottage cheese cartons to plain and shallow clay pots. Plastic trays about five inches deep also make excellent starting boxes. Be sure to punch drainage holes in the container so excess water can escape.

You can also take cuttings from houseplants to get new plants for your miniature gardens. Sever strong stem cuttings from mature plants by using a sterile, sharp knife. (Run a match over the knife blade to sterilize it.) Trim off bottom leaves, and dip the cuttings in hormone powder. Then set cuttings into a sterile potting mix (such as perlite or vermiculite) in clay pots, aluminum baking tins, or other suitable containers. Water soil lightly, and provide warmth and humidity. When seedlings show true leaves, the plants can be removed.

Still another way to get new plants is to take leaves from houseplants, for example, African violets. Place the severed leaves into a sterile potting mix and water them. Provide humidity and warmth. A Baggie or a similar plastic material over

To be sure cuttings of plants root properly, insert them in a plastic bag of vermiculite. The plastic bag provides adequate humidity. *(Photo by USDA)*

the propagating box will help provide humidity. When leaves appear, new plants can be placed in separate pots.

You can also use the process of division to get new plants. Division is merely separating mature plants that have several crowns. Run a sterile knife through the crowns; pot each division separately. Plants that grow in clumps, like ferns, are ideal subjects for division. From one you get two and in the process also help the mother plant: The surgery promotes new roots and growth.

Bromeliads and orchids produce youngsters at the base of the crown. These small plants, called offshoots or offsets, can be severed from the mother plant when they are three to four inches tall. Pot them in fir bark; eventually they will become replicas of their parent. Takes as much of the root system of the new plant as you can when you serve offshoots.

142

This Christmas cactus can be propagated by using a division of the plant as show. This should be rooted in vermiculite to furnish a new plant in time. *(Photo by author)*

Fledgling Care

Once you have the young plants on their own, follow some basic culture "rules" to help you help them become strong and healthy. As noted, some cuttings are put into a starter mix and then in soil, or, in the case of offshoots, set directly into soil. Once plants are in the permanent growing medium—a soil mix—give them a little more attention. Observe to see

Cuttings can be started in an incubator-type propagating box. When several inches high they should be potted in individual containers for room use. *(Photo by Matthew Barr)*

whether they are growing or merely surviving. Keep the soil evenly moist and temperatures about 75F during the day; 65F at night is fine.

Occasionally spray leaves with water to ensure good humidity and wipe foliage with a damp cloth now and then so leaf pores are always clean. Keep plants out of drafts or extreme heat. In other words, baby your young plants a little until they are really growing (fresh new growth of leaves and stems). Within a year the plant should be reaching its peak of form. If that gift plant of last year has not survived (even after reading this book), you will still have another one in its place.

11

Special Arrangements with Gift Plants

Gift plants can decorate any room and add beauty to the area, but there are still other ways to use these plants to great advantage indoors. Interesting table arrangements can be made with some of the plants, small garden groupings is another idea, and you can even have cut flowers from your gift plants. All these are bonuses when you tend plants carefully so they are with you for a long time.

Table Arrangements

African violets are popular plants principally used as window decoration, but because of new improved varieties that have abundant bloom, they can also star as centerpiece arrangements on the dining-room table. However, there are some tricks involved in accomplishing this end; you simply do not plunk a violet on the table and create a stellar centerpiece. Instead, use a suitable container such as a handsome brass planter twenty or twenty-six inches long, with three pot plants inside. This arrangement creates a colorful mass of flowers and is excellent for the dining table because it is low and does not obstruct vision. Set an inch of gravel in the container, and then place potted plants on top so that the pot rims are level

145

This simple table arrangement of cyclamens is most effective as a center-piece. *(Photo by Max Eckert)*

with the top of the container. Now add sphagnum moss around the pot rims to camouflage them: you have an instant floral arrangement for your table.

Pepper plants placed at varying levels on the table create unique table centerpieces. Find suitable one-, two-, and three-inch wooden blocks, and set one pot on each block to create a tiered effect. Now camouflage the blocks by arranging sheaths of dried wheat or bundles of dried flowers randomly around the pots. You can also use several large red apples in place of dried flowers.

Cyclamens also make handsome centerpieces. A group of red or pink cyclamens can create a harvest of color in quick order. Place the pots in suitable cover-ups or cachepots (see Chapter 2) and set them in a triangle on the table. Not much will be needed for this arrangement. Cyclamens are naturally leafy plants and need no other adornment. By themselves they are fine accents.

Hibiscus flowers can be used in a new way to dress a table. Select full blossoms and cut them where the base of the flowers joins the stem. Float two or three large flowers in water in a smart crystal bowl. They will last through the evening and add great flair to a table setting. Cutting the flowers does not harm the plant; indeed, it encourages new buds to form.

Cut Flowers

Orchids make splendid cut flowers and will last for days in a bowl or vase of water. Cut the flowers when they are fully open, taking as much stem as possible. Use a simple glass vase and arrange three or five blooms at varying levels in the water. With orchids, no accompaniment is necessary—they are dramatic flowers that can stand on their own beauty. Orchids can be used on a bedside table, in the hall, or wherever you want a touch of elegance.

Chrysanthemums, too, can be used in small bouquets in simple containers to dress an area with color. Arrange these as you would any cut flowers, and add some leafy greens to complement the blooms.

Here, cut flowers from gift plants are used with other flowers for a pleasing bouquet. *(Photo by Matthew Barr)*

For a very exotic arrangement you might want to use cut anthurium flowers, but these have to be carefully arranged to really look handsome. Use three to five flowers. Put some florist clay at the bottom of the container, and place stems so flowers are at varying heights. As with chrysanthemums, the anthuriums will need some leafy greens. If you have an asparagus fern in the house, cut a few branches and add them to the setting.

148

A simple but lovely arrangement of cut flowers for the table. *(Photo by Matthew Barr)*

Bulbs such as narcissus and hyacinth are of course not rightly cut flowers, but they can be used in containers as substitutes for them wherever you need a spot of color or something different. White narcissus are especially appealing, hyacinths always look lovely, and lots of small crocus can also be used to decorate an area.

Index

151

153